MW01290785

JOURNEY TO DATA SCIENTIST

JOURNEY TO DATA SCIENTIST

INTERVIEWS WITH MORE THAN TWENTY
AMAZING DATA SCIENTISTS

Kate Strachnyi

© 2017 Kate Strachnyi
All rights reserved.
ISBN-13: 9781548984243
ISBN-10: 1548984248

Dear Reader,

First of all, thank you for picking up this book! My name is Kate Strachnyi, and I am excited to share some interesting stories with you.

I've recently become obsessed with data science and the processes of applying a scientific method to answer the questions concealed in various forms of data. I was inspired to better understand these methods and ways I could master this incredible field.

In my pursuit of data enlightenment, I signed up for various tutorials and training sessions with sites, such as Lynda.com and Coursera. I started reading blogs, signed up for Kaggle competitions, and attended several meet-ups in my local area (NYC).

Overall, I found the culture within the data science community to be very inviting and welcoming of new members who shared similar levels of inquisitiveness.

I have always been compelled by a desire to derive meaning where otherwise none seemed to exist and quickly learned that the simple task of building a visual representation was an effective way to establish order from the chaotic frenzy of complex data fields.

To put it simply, where most see chaos, I see beauty. A beauty that only unfolds when we're able to tame those vast complexities and allow for a story to be told. A story without ambiguity and ripe with absolution and truth. A story, by data.

I started a blog called storybydata.com and a YouTube channel, Story by Data, to track my journey to data scientist, as well as to share my knowledge of data science.

I thought it would be really interesting to talk to experts in the field, so I began to speak to data scientists and noted down words of wisdom. I believe that there are others like me out there—people wondering about how to break into the data science field, who would love to hear from experts. Therefore, I decided to write this book!

My goal is to make the data scientist role more accessible to the public. The advice that I have is as follows: don't be deterred by thinking that there are too many barriers for entry (PhD, and so on). People took various paths to obtain the coveted title of data scientist.

Do you want to be a data scientist? Continue reading to gain amazing insights and career advice from over twenty data scientists from companies such as IBM, Bloomberg, Springboard, and Honeywell. These data scientists come from different industries and countries. One common theme that came out of all interviews is that in order to be successful, you must be innately curious. Never stop asking questions of the data, and never be satisfied with the results.

This book is dedicated to all aspiring data scientists.
Stick with it and you'll get there!

ACKNOWLEDGMENTS

Thank you to my mother for watching my two little girls as I juggled my responsibilities of motherhood, a full-time job, obtaining a data science certificate from Johns Hopkins (Coursera), and creating content for my *Story by Data* blog and YouTube channel. Thank you to my husband for pitching in when I needed to meet my writing goals and for believing in me.

Most of all, thank you to all the interview participants for making time in their busy schedules to have a conversation or correspond in support of this work. Your input has truly made this book what it is.

Data Scientist

A quick definition of a data scientist—a person who possesses several key skills and knowledge, including proficiency in mathematics, statistics, programming, and an understanding of his or her industry/domain. A data scientist must be able to think critically and solve problems that most people wouldn't dare to attempt. In fact, in a recent article, the *Harvard Business Review* identifies the profession as the "sexiest job of the 21st century."

A data scientist typically has some experience in working with large and/or messy data sets, being able to figure out how to address vague problems and come up with interesting insights from data, despite the sometimes-overwhelming volumes of it.

These characteristics are at the core of the data scientist and as you will soon learn from the following interviews, data scientists are innovators who are eager to think out of the box.

CONTENTS

RAJ BANDYOPADHYAY

Director of Data Science Education at Springboard

*"Often people tend to underestimate the business
and communication aspects of data science."*

Path to Data Science

I have an educational background in very traditional computer science. A bachelor's degree in computer science and a master's degree and PhD in computer science. I have worked in programming languages and compilers though it's very traditional computer science stuff. Graduated with a PhD in 2008 and started working as a developer at a start-up company in Atlanta. After working for three years, I realized that I wanted to do some data science software development while staying on in technology.

Considered something like management consulting, but I realized that I didn't want to; as much as I was interested in business, I wanted to remain close to technology, and I was not really interested in dedicating one hundred hours a week in consulting. This was the time Coursera launched its first course on machine learning. I took the course as it was kind of cool, and wanted to learn more about it. I started taking online courses, and began to change jobs, taking up jobs with more data engineering and data science roles. Eventually, ended up as the chief data scientist at a company called Pindrop Security, which is a security start up. I was the first and only data scientist. Eventually, over a period of two years, I built an entire data science team.

Later, I moved to San Francisco where my wife was working, so I quit my job in Atlanta. I was already mentoring for Springboard, so I took a full-time role with them to maintain and develop data science courses.

Selecting Candidates for Data Science Team

Pindrop Security is basically a machine-learning system used to detect fraud. In such a company, especially when it is a cyber-security company where the core product is based on data science, obviously, the technical knowledge has to be very high. The people you select, whether for transformation, internship, or on a contract basis have to be very good.

I hired three data scientists. One of them was a PhD in machine learning, so it was a very theoretical aspect for the group. The other two people had PhDs in aerospace engineering. One of them especially had experience in handling data as she had worked on data-related projects.

The third person had a master's in aerospace engineering and also an MBA—a very good combination of both technical knowledge and business skills.

The team had a broad set of skills with no fixed background. All of these people were very technically competent and had both engineering and math backgrounds. When I was hiring and interviewing people, there were two issues that I really found especially with fresh graduates: even those with data science degrees didn't have much experience with real-world data. So basically, though many of them had done projects as part of their courses, the projects were on data that was already cleaned up or data that was more toy data sets. They didn't have the experience of working on a data science project from scratch, figuring out how to collect the data, how to clean the data, what kind of data to collect and how difficult was the trade off in collecting different kinds of data. One criterion that I had was to look for candidates with experience in real-world data.

The other issue that I found in fresh graduates was that they weren't able to explain their projects to anybody outside the technical field; outside the data science field. Working as a data scientist in industry, whether it's in a small or in a big company, is not like an engineering role. It means as an engineer you work with the engineering team and do not need to explain to anyone outside your team or to the management.

However, whether you are a senior data scientist or a junior scientist manager, you have to interact with people in the sense that you are typically working with the product manager or the sales personnel or the marketing personnel: somebody who is outside your technical team and may not know anything about the work you do. What that means is you have to have really good communication skills to make them understand.

An Understanding of Business

You must be able to understand what business marketing is, what the salesperson is saying, and what their problem is. You must also be able to translate this into a data analysis problem. Then when you perform any kind of analysis that gives results, you have to explain it to them in the language they understand. You cannot say "90 percent true detection and 5 percent false positives", etc. You have to explain it and translate it into how much money they can make or how much more efficient the system can become.

This type of communication skill was really hard to find. So that was what I really tested for. I typically would ask them to take a project that they were working on or they had worked on, and explain it to someone in the room who was not a data scientist. I would take on the role of a management executive or a business manager or a product manager and they would have to explain it to me. What I really looked for in fresh graduates and people with experience was the ability to communicate what they had done.

Working with Messy Data—Springboard

At Springboard, we have data science courses that are data driven, and we also emphasize from the beginning that students have to work on a capstone project, because the guidelines for the actual projects for both mentors and students is that it has to be an interesting and realistic project.

What this means is that you start by coming up with a client. The idea is that even before you start working on the project you know this is the problem that I am going to solve and this is the client. For example, one of my students did a project where he would predict a landslide and the client would be the department of transportation who had to decide where to build roads.

We try to make projects as realistic as possible. We emphasize that students collect real-world data and it's not simulated data or collecting data from cases that are already clean. Then any kind of analysis they have to do themselves and come up with the presentation and report targeted at that client. So that's the approach that we take at Springboard to ensure that the students have the experience of the real-world data that helps them to learn how to clean up the abstract data and also have the experience of communicating with real-world clients.

Mentors at Springboard

All our mentors are active data scientists. There are people who work as data scientists as part timers or as contract employees, who bring industry perspective and can tell you what industry standards are basically.

When you hear a mentor telling you why you are doing something, you gain confidence in what you are doing and it helps you when you talk to other people who are experienced in data science and are looking for a job or some information in the field.

Spiked Number of Interest in Data Science

Interest and registration is definitely going up; recently, we launched a new program called data science career track—which is also called premium offer and it combines data science with job guarantee and career support. The number of applications for that was way more than we expected.

Interesting Project at Pindrop

At a project that I worked on in Pindrop Security, they had a system that analyses the audio of calls coming into a call center, which determines if the call might be fraudulent.

However, as part of being a data scientist especially in a company like that you probably have to speak about what are the data sources that you can analyze or that can add more color to the problem or what are the other methods that you can use.

There was this interesting problem that came to us from a client that was from banks, credit card companies, and other such companies. They said they had some interesting observations in their interactive voice response or IVR, which actually means automatic menus like press 1 to do this or to do that.

What they realized was that their IVR or what they suspected was actually that IVR had been attacked by the robot for code and it was trying out different combinations, in an attempt to guess combinations of account numbers and pins intending to extract customer information from that. When you have a bot, you can do millions of transactions a second. You can try several pins.

Imagine if there's a breach like what happened at Target or a bunch of credit card numbers or account numbers have been stolen and then they already have the pin. For those accounts, we can log in and get information about the accounts, which can be used in future attacks.

That's what they suspected; however, they didn't have a way to verify it and they also had no way to actually detect it. What they did was that they gave us data numbers for six months of IVR. I was the only data scientist at that point. I promised to do it. We took on that project and it took me about three months to cover the initial prototype and six months to come up with something that I could confidently say worked. Basically, I came up with a machine-learning solution to be able to verify the hypothesis. And there actually was that kind of pattern. The question we needed to solve was how to detect repeated attack patterns and how to separate that pattern from the regular users. It's difficult to distinguish between someone who forgot their pin number and was trying different combinations and someone who was attempting fraud. These are interesting questions that came up. We got a provisional patent on this.

Approach

I looked at the menu tree to learn what was the path followed for each call in the menu tree; then I extracted the features and added some labeled data initially about which calls are fraud and which calls are by the customers. Then I labeled certain calls as fraudulent or certain activities as fraudulent. And they have to come up with that classification and tell me how I will identify fraud.

Advice to Aspiring Data Scientists

People wonder if they should they have a master's degree or what credentials are important for the role. What I tell them is that what is most important for employers is having a good portfolio.

Projects show your technical competence and your communication skills. GitHub is important because it is the place for data scientists to show off their work. If you have a project on GitHub you will probably have documentation and write up for those projects, you will have a presentation and so on. That's what you show your potential employer and the potential employer or the data scientist will look at that and will say this person knows his or her stuff, how to communicate, how to present things and so on.

Ultimately, having a good portfolio is far more important than what kind of credentials or resume you have in data science even right now. I have noticed that when you work with a mentor where you give that kind of portfolio, you will be able to create projects that you are good at and add it to your portfolio. But you can do that on your own; ultimately what you want in your portfolio are realistic projects, which display your technical and communication skills.

Data Science Is a Combination of Skills

Data science is a combination of skills. It's an amalgamation of being a programmer, an algorithmic or a theoretical person, a statistical person, and a business person. Often people tend to underestimate the business and communication aspects of data science. They focus on the programming aspects: which language should I learn, or which algorithm should I learn. The communication and basics of business aspects are almost equally important to make or break your career in data science.

I urge people who want to take up data science not to underestimate the business and communication requirement in data science.

MATT WILLIAMS
CEO at WD Creative Analytics

"Data science is really COOL, and most people who work in this field care passionately about the work."

Path to Data Science

I took the long road, about fifteen years in Enterprise IT as an all-round data expert—first as a database engineer, then designed and built high-volume data integration systems at LexisNexis's legal information division, focusing on "fuzzy" match algorithms and understanding swarm approaches for processing large, unrelated data sets. Then, I moved to Analytics, insights, and strategy work for the last five years, so I am a "full stack" data scientist, comfortable loading, validating, and integrating data, then making sense of the consolidated picture, and surfacing key insights from there.

Changing Role of a Data Scientist

In the future, data science will change both from assembling data, to making sense of data. In the future, most data will be standardized, and some will be freely available and will auto-connect to external data sets without much human intervention. Today, we have to analyze for common components, and design an ETL (Extract—Transform—Load) or data loading process to link unrelated data sets together. In five to ten years, we'll use automated data linked applications that will find, validate, and link data for us.

Similarly, today, we have to write queries or review data visualizations to find key relationships, and in five to ten years, we will have automated processes that review data, and surface the insights and anomalies for us.

So the forward-looking data scientist will spend more time asking questions and testing hypotheses and less time merging data into a single picture or doing first-cut analysis to create initial hypotheses.

The data scientist in five to ten years will spend more time reviewing analyses, and validating automated conclusions that are machine-generated.

Reason for Getting into Data Science

I wanted to understand how our human knowledge is stored and validated and contribute to the development of artificial intelligence (AI). I studied cognitive science in college, and have always been interested in how humans map our knowledge into data systems. I've been leveraging models of cognition and human learning for my Enterprise IT data engineering projects ever since.

Typical Workday

Sometimes I meet customers to discuss new analytics projects in sentiment analysis, or AI-driven chat conversations, or streaming analytics from video and audio content.

Otherwise, I manage two teams—a team dedicated to building artificial intelligence systems. We meet in the morning to review our News streams, our Graph database development, and expand our Q+A capability to cover open-ended questions. Then, I have another team dedicated to pulling streaming metadata from Video and Audio, and using Python machine-learning libraries to find correlative patterns for engagement or conversion.

A Role Misunderstood

I think data science is best at identifying patterns across large data sets, and the best data science can remove/ignore any PII (personally identifiable information). I'm interested in how to extend and expand user data privacy while still advancing the practice of data science, especially machine learning.

Over time, these techniques will help keep everyone safer and more secure, and I think the opposite message is given to the public. Data science can be a huge contribution to a fairer, more transparent, and just society.

Also...data science is really *cool*, and most people who work in this field care passionately about the work.

HECTOR ALVARO ROJAS

DATA SCIENTIST AT SDP CONSULTING

"I see a huge growing expansion for the data science field and a huge global recognition of its immense importance for all humanity."

Path to Data Science

First of all, I call myself a "data scientist" but it is just a kind of brand designation. My knowledge is always adapting whether I am learning, complementing, or actualizing about different methods, tools, or applications frequently used in the data science field.

Remember that data science is considered as an "interdisciplinary field about processes and systems to extract knowledge or insights from data." Data science employs techniques and theories from many fields like statistics, mathematics, informatics, and computer science, among others. So, I think that instead of "being" a "data scientist," we are basically "living" in a beautiful field named "data science." You have to fight every day to be alive, and that fight implicitly involves a huge "help" to all humankind. That's what makes me happy, after all.

I view the field of data science as a natural continuation of the journey from the statistics field. I am constantly expanding myself in both fields, more so in data science, of course. I am expanding in a process that will take me forever, until the end of my human life.

Changing Role of a Data Scientist

I see a huge growing expansion for this field and a huge global recognition of its immense importance for all humankind. I see data science directly affecting—in a good way—industry, education, health, engineering, governments, and so on. So I recommend to all people to make their best effort to learn as much as they can about the beautiful "data science" field.

Typical Workday

Well, these days I am working as a freelance consultant as well as a part-time professor [statistics and math], so a regular day involves a lot of computer and statistics improvements, such as learning about big data processing and communication, new languages like Python, some fascinating R-projects packages for data processing and analytics, and things to further aid for visualization. The rest of my time is dedicated to eating, sleeping, physical exercises (which I love), looking for consulting opportunities, and whatever else that can be added to complete my twenty-four-hour day.

A Role Misunderstood

Much of the data scientist's capabilities are misunderstood these days. This is a generational problem. For example, some people are still reluctant to embrace the computer age, and so they are almost blind to all the advantages that computer technology brings to all humankind. Also, some may understand the computer's abilities, but they refuse to use it in their fields for even the most basic support.

Another situation can appear from people who are confused about the potentiality of some relatively new computer platforms or the data science field itself. I think this is a natural reaction for some groups of people when it comes to confronting something they do not know well instinctively, so they stay within their comfort zones.

At the same time, we can consider the fact that there exists limited accessibility for many people of poor and undeveloped countries, and for such systems to extract knowledge or insights from regular and big data is simply impossible.

Finally, I think that data science is presently, and for the foreseeable future, a most important field to contribute to the development and advancement of the human being and the "data scientist job" as one of the more important ones in helping humankind reach new goals.

MIKE TAMIR

CHIEF DATA SCIENTIST AT INTERTRUST TECHNOLOGIES CORPORATION

"Things break down when you are doing actual machine learning projects. Knowing what is going on in the coding side and knowing what is going on in the mathematical side is the difference between blindly wandering around trying to problem solve or actually knowing how to fix the problem."

Path to Data Science

When I was in graduate school, there were not really any formal data science training programs, so like many other people who become data scientists, I completed a technical graduate degree in another field and then migrated over. Mine was a multidisciplinary program at the University of Pittsburgh. I got a master's in the mathematics department and then in the physics department but I was actually getting my Ph.D. in the philosophy department, focusing on technical philosophy of physics. That's what I ended up writing my dissertation on—areas of general relativity and quantum statistical mechanics.

As I was finishing up I grew interested in machine learning, and coding in general. With the machine-learning background, I got a role out here to the Bay Area building up a "data science" lab. Back then the term "data scientist" was a completely new title (to be honest I didn't know what it officially meant at first). We built up a team with people from a diverse set of technical backgrounds, but few (myself included) had any formal computer science or machine-learning degrees. Now people go into computer science because machine learning is very hot, but it wasn't really a focus of all computer science programs back then.

Learn Mathematics and Statistics

It was my job for several years to think about learning statistics as part of becoming a data scientist. Statistical understanding really impacts the level of data science you are going to be able to do. I encourage anyone looking to become a top data scientist to cultivate a wide scope of skills in this area.

Mathematical literacy, such as understanding linear algebra, is likewise important. It really gives you a deeper insight into what you are doing. Things break down when you are doing actual machine learning projects. Knowing what is going on in the coding side and knowing what is going on in the mathematical side is the difference between blindly wandering around trying to problem solve or actually knowing how to fix the problem.

It's a defining marker of data science candidates when they can speak competently about core concepts in statistics and mathematics. The heart of what most data scientists do now is the machine learning, but understanding the mathematics and statistics underneath is critical for a data scientist to be successful.

Learn Machine Learning

Thinking about how machine learning is applied in industry directly influenced how we ultimately designed the master's program and redesigned the Zipfian data science boot-camp after we acquired them at Galvanize.

Modern expectations are that a data scientist understand core machine learning as table stakes. Presently, even entry level data scientists are expected to understand common tools for doing distributed machine learning at scale. As the way that data science integrates with engineering and production becomes more streamlined, that expectation is going to continue to harden.

Similarly, deep learning in industry has fast become reality as we continue to evolve with the hardware, machinery, and algorithms. One area of change that has been really impressive to me is the progress that has been made in natural language processing (NLP) using neural networks. The creation of neural embedding techniques combined with recurrent neural networks has really changed the game of what's possible when working with text. We can now train algorithms to solve problems like text summarization, translation, and even fake news detection in ways that were not possible when I first got started. This is a promising area that deep learning will hopefully continue to revolutionize.

ALEXANDER BESSONOV

Data Scientist at Bloomberg LP

"Reframe your mind to be data driven: look at the
businesses around you and try to guess (or read)
how they solve their problems with data science,
and how you think it can be improved."

Path to Data Science

It was when I was working for a data warehousing company, where I was writing a lot of (pretty complex) SQL queries and had a pretty vague title (professional services consultant), when I noticed that data science and machine learning began to appear in many news articles. I started researching the area and in about six months I started looking for data science projects within my company. After two more years, I changed jobs (and country of residence) and became a manager in the Decision Analytics department. The idea of the hiring manager there was to hire people with knowledge of open source big data stack and experience with programming languages like Python and R. But since they were an SAS shop, they weren't able to find projects for me and wanted to make me switch to the dark side and learn SAS instead. After about eight months I left and got my official title of data scientist.

Data Scientist Qualities

The term "data scientist" means different things to different companies. Some hire people with knowledge of statistics and basic knowledge of

R, others require knowledge of intricacies of ML algorithms and distributed systems. In my own opinion, a data scientist is a person who, if given a business problem, can find a working hypothesis, jump in, and build a working prototype. This obviously requires either a good team of engineers who could help, some sort of self-service platform, or a unicorn who can do everything.

Changing Role of a Data Scientist

I think the role will be divided into well-formed job descriptions, which clearly define specifics of the problems the person is supposed to solve. Main changes will be in the tools we use. There are already a lot of tools that allow performing (literally) drag and drop analysis. The problem with them is that they are not mature enough to be used in production. Obviously, new machine-learning algorithms and visualization tools will appear. The hardware will also change, probably many devices will have some chips specifically designed to perform neural network computations (separate from GPUs or "graphics processing units").

Advice for Aspiring Data Scientists

Learn multiple programming languages, SQL. Reframe your mind to be data driven: look at the businesses around you, and try to guess (or read) how they solve their problems with data science, and how you think it can be improved. Practice on Kaggle, your own toy problems, or with the data you have at work.

MANSI GUPTA

Data Scientist at LinkedIn

*"It is no secret that most companies rely on data
to aid strategy and decision making."*

Path to Data Science

I pursued my undergraduate degree in computer science from Birla Institute of Technology and Science, Pilani, and graduated in 2015. During graduation, I pursued electives such as machine learning and advanced data science and projects related to information retrieval, social media mining, and machine-learning techniques, which initiated me into the field of data science. At this time, this is something that used to excite me but I wasn't sure about making data science as a career. In the summer of 2014, I secured internship in LinkedIn in their Systems and Networking team. This was the time when I started exploring online courses on Coursera and saw the lectures of the famous Andrew Ng's machine-learning course. I learned Python and tried to solve problems on Kaggle independently but didn't succeed in completing any solution. During this time, I explored different teams in the company and the one that allured me the most was the Search team.

I did another internship in LinkedIn in my final semester in the Search team. This team works on various "verticals" of LinkedIn searches, such as searches on companies, universities, articles, internal LinkedIn code, Slideshare, and Lynda (videos and courses). During the internship, I built a system to detect near-duplicate articles on LinkedIn to weed out plagiarized articles. I liked the work of the team and got accepted in a full-time role as a software engineer. I worked on the whole lifecycle of a query, from query understanding to serving users meaningful search results. As this was a software engineering role, I had to deal with a lot of search infrastructure related stuff instead of pure data science. This experience helped me a lot in knowing about how systems work at scale, state-of-the-art practices in information retrieval, dealing with multi-language data and troubleshooting infrastructure problems.

After working for one and a half years in the team (six-month internship and one-year full-time role), I wished to solve research oriented problems in natural language processing (NLP) and machine learning (ML).

I explored opportunities in various research oriented companies like IBM, Xerox Research, Adobe Research, and research fellowships in universities in India like IIT Bombay, IIT Kanpur, and IISc, Bangalore. But the most exciting opportunity presented in LinkedIn itself through a new "Spam and Relevance" team.

I was an active participant in LinkedIn Bangalore's Machine Learning Reading group during my role as the software engineer. This, along with my previous related work, helped me to get accepted in the Spam and Relevance team as an applied research engineer / data scientist, which is my current role.

As a team, our objective is to throttle the generation and spread of spam and unprofessional and low-quality content on LinkedIn. We build machine-learning-based models to classify spam, predict virility, and improve feed quality. I am currently working on an interesting project aimed at quantifying the tendency of LinkedIn members to spread low-quality content on LinkedIn network and analyzing graph structure on the basis of this quantification (score).

A Basic Data Science Framework

Regarding learning machine learning and data science, courses in the university and Coursera provided a basic framework in my mind. Apart from that, I mostly learn during the day-to-day work by reading research papers, watching video lectures pertaining to the topic I am working on, reading blogs, and reading relevant chapters of books from renowned professors.

Why I Got into Data Science

From a very young age, I've been highly sensitive toward social evils like violence against women, global issues like widespread hunger, climate change, and so on. The potential impact on masses is what motivates me to get up and work every day. I wish to contribute in solving these problems through my work. I realized that machine learning and natural language processing are central in tackling numerous high-impact social problems. For instance, ML and NLP are being used to detect deception using linguistic and physiological features

It is no secret that most companies rely on data to aid strategy and decision making. Sophisticated algorithms govern even the miniscule bits of information presented on our screens. But in developing countries like India, public institutions, whose policies affect the life of millions of people, have only begun to realize the value of leveraging data. There lies a huge potential in solving the most critical global problems through data-driven technologies. In future, I envision myself as an industry or academic researcher working with government, civic and nonprofit organizations using technology to augment human discernment to bridge this gap.

This potential of impact was an important factor for me to choose data science. And my interest in the field only helped to decide. Now, in my current team I work with prominent researchers in the field who are PhDs or/and have significant experience in data science. Here, I realize the limitations of my knowledge on a daily basis. To address this, I have decided to pursue a master's degree in computer science focused on machine learning from a reputable university in United States, starting in the fall of 2017. I might continue into a PhD program, have my own start-up or work in industry, depending on what best fulfills my above-mentioned goal.

Typical Workday & Tools Used

At LinkedIn, I work from about 9:00 a.m. to 6:00 p.m. from Monday to Friday. I realized that data cleaning, standardization, and preprocessing take a lot of time (days or even months) before I actually start to build ML models. And since the work is "research" (for lack of a better word)

in nature, there are instances when there is nothing much to be gleaned from the data after a lot of grunt work you have put in. The key is not to be disappointed and hope for the law of averages to work. Sometimes the insights are so motivating, that you wish to share them to the world. For instance, we have submitted our recent analysis on LinkedIn network in the International Conference on Web and Social Media (ICWSM).

I primarily use Pig for data processing, Python for building models, and Java for deploying the models into production.

Also, I recently joined as a Freelance Technical Writer for the blog of the company SocialCops (blog.socialcops.com). Their vision of solving critical problems through data resonates with me. I work on making sense of the civic data and providing insights.

KUNAL JAIN

FOUNDER & CEO AT ANALYTICS VIDHYA

"I increasingly see people thinking that once they know how to code an algorithm, they are a data scientist."

Path to Data Science

I graduated from the Indian Institute of Technology (IIT), Bombay, in 2006 and got placed at Capital One as part of our campus placement. I wouldn't say that I knew what I was getting into. But I always knew what I did not want to do. So I skipped some of the popular companies in the placement process and ended up joining Capital One, as the role sounded exciting. I always enjoyed numbers, statistics, coding, and applied Mathematics—so the role looked like a good fit.

I had a great time and learned a lot at Capital One. It was probably one of the best places to start my career. I learned about the values and the ecosystem required to foster innovation. Capital One had a thriving community of some of the best business analysts I know. Then, in 2010, I decided to come back to India as I wanted to be in India in the long term. I joined an Insurance company that was looking to set up an Analytics team. In the next four years, we scaled this two-member team to a team of twenty people.

During this period, the need to have an ecosystem for analytics and data science professionals kept coming back. I could not find any place where I could go and ask questions about analytics and data science to other people. I had to rely on my friend's professional circle for any brainstorming or to understand any tools and techniques. We had to go through research papers to understand how some of the algorithms worked. That is when I thought that having a community of analytics and data science professionals would help everyone.

Started with a Blog

I had no clue how to build such a niche community (this was 2013). So I started by creating a personal blog. I thought that I should start by sharing my learning and my perspective. If people found it useful, they might contribute and maybe we could create a community then. Interestingly, people started following my blog, and they started asking questions through comments. People liked what I was writing, and the blog started becoming popular. Over the next six months, I began to realize the kind of impact I could create through a community like this. It became much more exciting than my day job. I decided to pursue "Analytics Vidhya" full time.

My family was always supportive of what I wanted to do, and we had some savings to give "Analytics Vidhya" a shot. In 2014 I started doing Analytics Vidhya full time, and we transformed this blog into a community of analytics and data science professionals. Today, we run a community-driven blog, a discussion portal, a hackathon platform, a jobs portal, several meet-ups, and webinars for our community members. We are one of the largest data science knowledge portals and communities in terms of registered users and visitors on the site.

We continue to stay true to our vision of creating a knowledge portal for analytics and data science professionals and want to make this a preferred destination for our community members. We hope that by understanding them better, we will be able to serve them even better.

Data Scientists Skills and Personality Type

I would say that an ideal data scientist should possess three broad categories of skills:

The first one is analytical and technical skills. This includes knowledge of mathematics, statistics, coding, structured thinking, data engineering, and other data hacking skills. The second set includes soft skills like curiosity, communication skills, influencing and presenting skills, and people perseverance. The final set of skills includes business domain knowledge, understanding business processes, and knowing the problems that the business is facing.

The challenge is that it is very difficult to find someone with all these skills. You might not even find any people with these skill sets. So if I have to pick critical skill sets that I look for hiring, I go for structured thinking, curiosity, and very high motivation. I believe that if these skills are in place, you can build on other skills. If these are missing, they are difficult to build on.

Changing Role of a Data Scientist

The honest answer is that it is very difficult to make predictions over a long horizon. The technology and landscape is changing so quickly that it is hard to imagine what the next five to ten years have in store. Having said that, here are a few trends I can see:

The amount of data generation is going to continue to increase at an exponential pace. Internet of Things (IoT) and connected devices are going to be major drivers of this. Think of it like this—today some of the biggest data sets come from studying online consumer behavior—Google and Facebook are leading this. Websites and applications today can track every action, every click, and hence the underlying behavior. Most of the people don't realize how granular and information rich this data is. Now imagine, if the physical world can be traced and tracked with similar accuracy. How do you sleep? How do you spend your day? Whom do you meet and where? How frequently? All of this would get tracked in the years to come.

Machine-based computations will continue to evolve and become stronger. Increase in the granular data combined with new algorithms, cheap storage and computational resources will unleash unseen benefits and threats to humankind. We will be able to solve problems we never thought machines were capable of. Machines will first become companions and start replacing mundane jobs as we start getting more and more data. Analytics and data science will become a differentiator for more and more businesses.

With these changes going around, you will need a different skill set in today's workforce. You would need more and more people to be comfortable with data engineering and analysis skills. You will need people who could make sense of data at scale. Hence, I believe that companies would need to up-skill/reskill their management to have the necessary data science skills. Managers with understanding of data science would be equivalent to MBAs in the last decade.

Career Accomplishments

I would say that it is greatly satisfying and fulfilling that our work at Analytics Vidhya is impacting millions of people every month. We have seen hundreds of people who achieved success and realized their dreams using the resources on Analytics Vidhya.

In hindsight, it might seem like an easy call to build a community in analytics and data science. But at the start, I had no idea what shape and form Analytics Vidhya would take. I could have stayed in a well-paying corporate job, but it could have taken many more years before I could have created a similar impact. I am glad that I heard what my heart said and followed it instead of analyzing the situation too much!

Projects

I have worked in markets/geographies/companies with different levels of maturity, and accordingly the challenges have been very different.

While I was in the United Kingdom working for a bank, the challenge was to be innovative and to come up with ways in which data could be more useful. This included reading about new techniques, identifying problems, and then solving them using your own set of hypothesis and data. Since the organization was already established, a lot of data was in place by then.

When I came back to India in 2010, the challenges were entirely different. We created a small team within our organization and the task was to provide how analytics and data could add value. This involved identifying what data might be available, going out and collecting it, cleaning it to make it useful, and at the same time keeping the stake-holders excited about what analytics could do.

Advice to Aspiring Data Scientists

These are very exciting times to be in this domain. The domain is expected to grow and grow fast in coming years. The first thing you should do is make sure that this is the place you want to be in. As a person, do you have the required curiosity? Do you enjoy slicing and dicing data? Do you enjoy unearthing complex relationships and putting them to use?

If you do, then data science is the right field for you. A few other things to keep in mind during the early days:

Pick one tool and focus on learning that one tool only. A lot of people try and learn multiple tools early in their careers. More often than not, it ends up hurting them. You can choose any popular language/tool and it would have everything you would need as a data scientist. The best companies today hire for problem solving skills and not for knowledge of the tools

Focus on fundamentals rather than on code. Again, I increasingly see people thinking that once they know how to code an algorithm, they are data scientists. I have seen people doing really well in competitions struggling to even frame a data science problem from a business problem. In real life, you do not get to train and test data readily, and the way to define the problem can have high influence on the outcome.

Apply your learning to real-life problems—pet projects, data science competitions, and hackathons are some ways to do that. Last but not the least—keep learning!

KHALIFEH AL JADDA, PhD

LEAD DATA SCIENTIST AT CAREERBUILDER

*"A good data scientist is one that works on iterations
and communicates findings after each iteration to
get feedback before moving to the next iteration."*

Data Science in the South

I spoke at many data science and big data conferences in 2016; none
of those conferences took place in any of the southern states. As a
data scientist from the southern data science community, I felt that
our community is behind its counterpart communities on the West and
East Coasts. Southern Data Science Conference (www.southerndatasci-
ence.com) is an attempt to bridge that gap between our southern data
science community and the ones on the East and West Coasts.

Since this is the very first data science conference in Atlanta, I have
to deal with many challenges that range from bringing top speakers
from the top companies on the West Coast like Google, Microsoft, and
Groupon, to finding sponsors who would invest money to promote their
brands in the South. However, with the network I have built by speaking in the data science conferences, I was able to get top speakers from
the best companies, research centers, and schools. On the other hand,
the great support from the southern tech companies like CareerBuilder,
Macy's Technology, and LexisNexis solved the sponsorship issue.

Interesting Project

In 2005, I did my master's thesis on data mining, which was at that time an emerging field in computer science. The work I did in my master's thesis made me so interested in this research field. When I started my PhD program at the University of Georgia (UGA), I had to work on Glyco-Informatics projects, which aim to help understanding the relationship between the Carbohydrate (Glycans) and cancer. That kind of research is very useful, and I felt passionate about it; yet, I was trying to connect that domain with my interest in machine learning and data mining.

Luckily, I was able to find a very interesting problem, which is recognizing the glycan's structure from the mass spectrometry data as a good use case of applying machine learning on a large scale. I proposed a new probabilistic graphical model (PGMHD) called a new machine-learning model for that use case and for any huge hierarchical data.

In the meantime, I got an internship with CareerBuilder within the search technology group. CareerBuilder gave me a great opportunity to start my career as a data scientist when they assigned me as an intern on an R&D project to start building the back end of a new semantic search engine. I got a chance to work on really big data including billions of search logs, millions of resumes, and millions of job postings. That work on semantic search was the beginning of my career as a data scientist, and I still owe the success I have today in my career to that opportunity.

I'm so proud of my contribution to the search relevancy and recommendation domain. The techniques and algorithms I published with my team in that domain have been recognized by the data science community, and many colleagues find them useful in practice. I think what makes our work useful in practice is the fact that we publish the techniques that we applied successfully on really big data sets, which we have access to via CareerBuilder.

Evolving Role of a Data Scientist

I see the data scientist role evolving in five to ten years from focusing on building and scaling up machine-learning algorithms to finding new interesting use cases for these models. With the current pace of building open source machine-learning libraries and packages and making them available to everyone via cloud platforms, data scientists will no longer need to focus on implementing machine-learning models or inventing new ones. The competition will be in finding interesting use cases to apply those available models on the massive data sets, which will be available to reveal new findings or insights. With a revolution in the Internet of Things (IoT), data scientists will be focused more on connecting the dots, and working on how to integrate the data collected from everywhere to extract valuable insights and information that add value to people's lives and businesses.

An Effective Data Scientist Delivers Value

A good data scientist is one who delivers value. In the industry, many companies complain that their data scientists don't add value to the business. This problem usually happens when the data scientist focuses on solving interesting complicated problems using sophisticated machine-learning models without consideration of the business need. Therefore, a good data scientist should understand what value he can bring to the business given the data he has access to; moreover, he should be able to communicate the value of his work to the business leaders in the language that they understand. Also, a good data scientist is one who iterates his work; it is a very common mistake that data scientists isolate themselves working on a problem for months without communicating and sharing their findings. A good data scientist is one who works on iterations and communicates findings after each iteration to get feedback before moving to the next iteration and also one who has mathematical and statistical knowledge, coding skills, critical thinking, machine-learning knowledge, and communication skills.

Advice for Aspiring Data Scientists

My advice to anyone interested in becoming a data scientist is to not give up. The demand for data scientists will keep growing in the coming years, so we need more people to enter this domain. With the massive online resources available today for free that teach the basics and technologies used in data science, you only need passion and commitment. I would recommend learning the following:

1. Scripting language (Python or R)
2. SQL
3. machine learning (basics)
4. Apache Spark

Once you have these technical skills, start playing with really big data sets, which you can access for free on Kaggle (www.kaggle.com). That should make you a hot candidate in data science.

SERGEY BRYL

Data Scientist at MacPaw Inc.

> *"I believe that a good Data Scientist is always in good shape*
> *regarding modern data mining techniques, programming*
> *and data visualization, is able to understand the real needs*
> *of the business, provide recommendations to meet those needs,*
> *and speaks in a simple language when describing a solution*
> *(even if he is tempted to use long sentences like this)."*

Path to Data Science

I had an early romance with math and programming since school, and later on, at the university. I had obtained a degree in Finance 10 years before the term "Data Science" was coined and 15 years before it turned into a buzz-word. That's why my path is probably different from the traditional one when a scholar pursues their once chosen specialty.

For a long time, I successfully worked at a bank. I have always been drawn to numbers and analysis and had roles as Head of the Analytics and Risk Management departments. Years of experience and financial crises revealed to me that banks present themselves as conservative, reliable, and innovative but in fact, they are not. I was losing motivation, so I started looking into opportunities in analytics and other arenas.

One such opportunity was the job as a marketing analyst in the US-based company Namecheap. I learned a new scope and tools and always tried to suggest things beyond of what was requested.

So eventually, when working on one of such concepts about forecasting customer lifetime value, I realized that my main instrument i.e. Excel was by its very design incapable of solving the problem. At that time we had 1.5 million of clients whose transaction data spanned back 7-8 years. I started seeking the alternative instruments that would allow me to process that enormous data and crack the issue. This is what brought me to R language with its absolute freedom of actions, diverse possibilities, and impressive visualization.

I had to struggle my way through it at first. It took me hours to find and do simple things that earlier took just minutes to do in Excel. But the speed of processing the volumes of data was nowhere near Excel. R processed within seconds what Excel required hours to swallow. Such an immense potential solidified my confidence to go further. With time, I managed to write R scripts faster than Excel formulas and I switched to R completely, making it my major weapon. This is how my path is Data Science started.

In those days there weren't many R-related materials around. That's why I decided to contribute to the R community when possible. I started popularizing R via my personal blog, analyzecore.com by simply describing real-life cases I was dealing with.

Writing my own articles helped me grow professionally because you have to learn every bit of your subject before explaining it to others. The readers (data freaks from around the world), eventually liked the practical slant of my articles. I also supported them with simple and handy visuals, which everybody enjoyed. Surprised I was when my blog became somewhat popular, even despite the fact that the first articles were "unprofessional" at best.

Qualities of a Good Data Scientist

The existing variety and pace of development of the data analysis sphere makes it almost impossible to keep up with all developments. That is why the data scientist profession entails the constant following, learning, and adaptation to the full range of opportunities in real life cases.

I believe that a good Data Scientist is always in good shape regarding modern data mining techniques, programming and data visualization, is able to understand the real needs of the business, provide recommendations to meet those needs, and speaks in a simple language when describing a solution (even if he is tempted to use long sentences like this).

Data Science Project

I have been lucky to work for great companies with great people I liked very much, including projects I have worked or are working on right now. I can't say that I like some projects better than others but I definitely can say that the types of projects that motivate me the most are those that greatly affect the business. I enjoy seeing how the business or product changes because of my research. From this point of view, the company I currently work for (MacPaw) is unique and I truly love to work there.

I can highlight a few recent projects that we did with the team:

- A multi-channel attribution model based on Markov chains (you can find it on my
- analyzecore.com blog). The model gives us a chance to adequately distribute value via all marketing channels, and adjust marketing budgets accordingly;
- An Anomaly Detection Project. It allows us to automatically detect anomalies through many metrics and dimensions. As a result, we get notified about these anomalies in Slack, which makes our life way easier;
- This year the company released a new subscription service, namely Setapp (setapp.com). The service offers a free 30-day trial. We introduced a model which tells us whether the user ultimately converts into a paid subscriber. This broadens the boundaries for us, as for example, we can assess the effectiveness of our promo campaigns earlier in the game. Now we don't have to wait till the trial is over to see what percentage of users convert into subscribers.

A Day in the Life of a Data Scientist

Typically, I work on one or occasionally two projects at a time. Every project has a unique destination and progress and this is why no working day can't be the same as the previous one. However, there are some things that I try to do regularly. I've designed the desired everyday schedule for myself:

- 3-4 "sprints" for 1h 20 mins of focused work on a project;
- 1 hour a day learning something difficult;
- reading some medium-level professional material during my way to the office.

Of course, such a schedule is difficult to adhere to all of the time, but I try my best to follow it. Also, I have a wonderful family, two sons. That's why all my non-working hours I devote to my family. There is also a bit of free time when everybody is asleep when I can learn new stuff, and occasionally, write for my blog, analyzecore.com.

Any words of wisdom for Data Science students or practitioners starting out?
Never stop learning and do what you really love!

DIANE REYNOLDS

Chief Data Scientist at IBM

"Usually when we are looking to employ data scientists, we look for a strong educational background, preferably a PhD or master's."

Path to Data Science

Just for some background—when I was in university, it was about the time when the first web browser was created, and so things like mobile phones didn't really exist yet. I think we might have had car phones back then. But personal computers—again, they probably existed, but they weren't prevalent. I think that is one of the important things to understand just because it changes some of the perspective on what I'm about to discuss.

I started studying actuarial science in the university, because both my parents where in that field of work. I thought they had interesting jobs, and I liked math. After a year or so in the university, I had to actually declare a major, and the way it works here in Canada is you join the department to begin with and then about halfway through your second year, you actually declare what you intend to graduate in specifically. The university I went to had mathematics, actuarial science, and computer science together in the same department.

I switched my degree to both actuarial science and computer science. I decided to do a degree in statistics and finance (master's). I took several PhD statistics courses, economics and portfolio management, and derivatives courses that year. Algorithmics was one of the sponsors for the program, and so they hired me right after school, in Toronto, where I worked in market risk.

At that time, I was helping clients view software to calculate value at risk, to evaluate different types of derivatives, to create scenarios, to project the economy going forward.

Then I moved into working on operational risk, which has different risk factors than market risks, and we had a lot of different data and different types of data. Also, it was a much more a procedural world. In 2003–2004, I moved into credit risks and then portfolio credit risk, where I looked at how economic factors affect companies and how companies are affected by common factors. I worked on this until I joined IBM.

Around 2003–2004 was the height of CDOs or collateralized debt obligations, credit derivatives. By 2011, I was helping other people understand risks. Your results are only as good as your data, which is something that we learned from the crisis as well as other things.

One of the risks was that there was no updated information on the models. All these approximations that were happening were supporting misdirection through analytics. I looked at the quality and reliability of data, and I worked on that project for about a year and a half.

I spent the next eighteen months looking at fintech and what was going on out there, using the combination of knowledge I had of financial data and how the sector works, paired with my statistics background. I decided to upgrade my skills by learning some of the new technology that the person I was shadowing was involved in, so then I took over a data scientist's team.

Data Science Team

Right now, we have about six people on the team. Some of them I've hired, some of them I have borrowed and added into the pool and then into the team. So over the last year, we probably had about a dozen different data scientists, but this year I have full-time data scientists that report to me.

Everything was new so what we would do is to take people who worked on a consulting project out into the field and bring them to work for me for a little while and then rotate them.

What It Takes to Be a Data Scientist

Generally, there are a few necessary mathematical skills a good data scientist needs to have, namely statistics, machine learning, some kind of queuing theory or operation research that would include optimization, and specialist role that would also include things like cryptography and mathematical algorithm. Knowledge of financial mathematics is a plus, as the derivatives pricing is part of statistics.

Usually when we are looking to employ data scientists, we look for a strong educational background, preferably a PhD or master's, with specialization in mathematics. The ability to apply it and to really understand the application because we work in the financial services sector, which usually means some exposure to the sector earlier in the course of their careers. Good communication skills are also essential. It's not a prerequisite; rather it's a necessity.

Recommendation for Coursera Courses

I found the Coursera Data Science courses to be really useful in getting an overview of what data science is, picking up some of the newer terminology, and also learning how to interpret the R language. I've programmed in thirty different languages so what I understand from Coursera is really...I can do this in the R language and get familiar with the standard libraries and that sort of thing. In that respect, it is very useful. I do think, however, that they kind of give the misleading impression that when you're done with it; you can call yourself a data scientist in the absence of everything else. The syllabus isn't encompassing enough to qualify you as one; it's a nice certificate in the end. But there's a lot of guessing that goes on whether or not you passed. I also think they have ongoing issues of plagiarism and so on because things get published on the Internet.

I think it's a no if you're confident in your statistics background; it's a great way to learn R and kind of see what the rest of the world is doing in data science right now, but I don't think it's good to teach programming or statistics, or in fact if they teach you enough about subjects to make you a data scientist.

Regulatory Requirements Parsing Project

It is an ongoing project for me, and our objective is to be able to pick a piece of regulation that will be broken down by the computer into a series of obligations that you have to follow to meet such regulation.

Any time you look into the regulation, basically the statement from the government about what must be done to comply with that regulation, what comes out of it is a series of obligations that must be met. That process given the amount of new regulations that come out yearly is ever growing, and a lot of it keeps getting updated.

Advice to Data Scientists

I guess at some point I said there's a list of qualifications that make a good data scientist, but I think the other important point for me is the personality of the person: you have to be curious enough to build data. Yeah, I said that it is the curiosity to find data to build and to be really committed to always work on new things. Commitment can be doing a course on Coursera or doing something to improve your knowledge of what's going on out there in the world. That continuous work you do will make you a better data scientist. There are lots of ways of doing it today: one of the things I actually do is online competitions (Kaggle).

VAIBHAV GEDIGERI

Data Scientist at Honeywell

"The data science field lacks diversity, and we need more women in this field. We really need more women stepping into this field."

Path to Data Scientist

I always wanted to get into artificial intelligence (AI). I enjoyed the courses I took on AI, and the best logical extension then was to pursue my master's degree in machine learning and applied logistics.

It started off in 2014, and my first breakthrough was actually with Professor Carlin Hafiz. He was looking for students with a little background in the AI space; he had a huge research project that was coming up. They were trying to hire research assistants.

Twitter Uncovers Depression

The project was focused on text mining, analyzing tweets. First, we realized that there are practically no clinical lab tests to test for depression. We wanted to experiment on looking at a person's social media activity (on a happiness scale of 1 to 10); could we pull a classifier to identify whether this person possesses signs of depression? The best part was that we could actually provide help or reach out to concerned people in advance and this could make a difference for people.

This was the very abstract idea we were working on. The first step really was to collect data and I feel that's where all this started: I think what we call data science has always been data manipulation, feature extraction, feature engineering. We needed a way to collect tweets, but again we needed to identify which tweets we would collect. We had to identify potential user groups, where people talk about depression and it varied.

We identified about five to ten potential user groups with a very high density of tweets, and that's when we tried to collect the data by using APIs, or application programming interfaces.

We were contacted by a company based in San Francisco called Ginger. io; the company was involved in a similar experiment. They have an application to track social media activity of a person and other statistics that they use to calculate and actually make informed decisions about the need to visit a doctor, and so on. They showed interest in our project and reached out offering to help us with the project. At this time, we were developing a methodology, but unfortunately it was the end of my time on that project.

This is the project that acted as a springboard for me; my first opportunity as a data scientist.

Pharmaceutical Forecasts

Another firm I worked with is focused on clinical intelligence. They collect clinical lab data of rare Genomic diseases, so it could be Acromegaly or even conditions such as Hepatitis C. They slice and dice the data to provide a 360-degree view to their clients (primarily pharmacy clients). Clients would make data requests such as—show us the data for Hepatitis C for specific time periods or for certain locations. We would forecast the number of positive cases for time periods.

The most interesting part about these questions is that they are marketing or business oriented questions. There are a series of tests every patient has to undergo. Not every person takes all the tests so this actually helps pharmaceutical companies to manage their drug supply. This is something that helps them in their supply chain management, sales, and marketing.

Tools & Software

Primarily, we used R and Tableau, created decision trees (machine learning). The best part was getting to play around with really large amounts of data. There were about forty to forty-five million records; we were using Amazon Redshift. I immediately noticed from my academic perspective that when you are at school the data that you use is basically static data.

Lacking Diversity

I see changes in not only the skills but also the diversity—there is a lack of diversity. I felt so happy when I read an article that Google hired two people, and they are female. I feel we lacked diversity in the previous organization where I worked. The data science field lacks diversity, and we need more women in this field. We really need more women stepping into this field.

Choosing the Employer

I had a few offers on the table. I'm currently working at a start-up within Honeywell. The best part about this is that we have an umbrella or support from the large organization.

When I walked in, the first thing I came to know was that apart from the data they already have (you know the rich data that they have), Honeywell itself is in several industries, and they have automatic control system, they have home building and technologies, they have performance material technologies, and so on.

I chose Honeywell because they had a product and data science that was revolving around that product, which was great.

Now I am working on multiple projects, and I am assigned to three clients, and the good thing about this is each of them has a very different perspective. Most of the data that we get to work with is sensor data, derived from Internet of Things (IoT). That is the worst possible data you want to work with, and that's the reason I decided to challenge myself.

The Future

I have seen several products that include sensors (such as thermostats, and lighting control). It's making life easier. People are progressing in their lives. No one wants to make an effort anymore. We want it all in that place. I love to come home and see my house at 70 degrees waiting for me; it's incredible. I control my lights and other things just from my phone.

We are in a very preliminary stage; and there could be some downsides to it all. Stephen Hawking has been pressing on this, saying that AI can backfire on humans. That's one of the biggest threats.

Google, Twitter, Bot

An example of how AI can backfire comes from when Google trained a Twitter bot to reply everyone on Twitter. During the 2016 presidential elections, the bot lost control. It started making very, very harsh statements. It started posting threats and racist comments. Google had to remove it straight away.

Ten years down the line we will have robots. What Stephen Hawking said is that if you make the robots so good, even if one of them goes out of control there will be no stopping it. These are the things that have to be kept in mind when it comes to AI, and machine learning. I think that's again a side that's much unexplored. People are not really thinking about it as yet.

Start with the Basics

It is important to start off with fundamentals. I started with two years of reading things such as mathematics and algebra. It actually helped me to understand the mechanism of how algorithms work. Maybe a lot of people argue that this is only really required if you are getting into academia; I find it to be necessary in all lines of data science work.

SEAN PREUSSE

LEAD ANALYST AT WESTPAC GROUP

"Trust is important in data science, you often need to balance both accuracy with explainability when dealing with predictions on the workforce."

Career Path

I come from a business background with a degree in HR. I wasn't sure what I wanted to do within HR but quickly found satisfaction in linking analytics to people strategies and working towards optimizing the workforce and creating a better employment experience.

Ten years later I am in the same role but there have been many advancements. The systems that collect information have become richer, data points collected about our employees have transitioned from operational intent to include a more strategic purpose.

We are still dealing with the same length of data i.e. 200,000 employees both active and separated with a history spanning 8+ years. Much smaller in comparison to other departments but I would say more challenging as it has become very wide over time i.e. Attributes across the employment life cycle, sensor data to understand health, email, social media and mobility that look at networks and working habits.

Questions asked from the data have evolved materially, they have moved from simple attrition rates, training compliance and engagement scores to complex, what are the drivers of employee separation, engagement, how is the quality of hiring impacting revenue or cost?

43

Seat at the table

HR has a large role to play within data science, the seat at the table exists as the workforce usually accounts for 40-60% of operating expense and CEOs are always looking to optimize cost whilst also balancing this with productivity and engagement. When compared to other data science teams we are usually closer to the CEO as well, with HR reporting directly which means we have both the opportunity and greater risk to present the right insights that provide a balanced view on the impact to the workforce.

Working for a large organization does help in creating the right models but it is also important to understand the employment context i.e. what industry segments do you operating in as you can be dealing with different behaviors within each group. Depending on this mix, smaller organizations with 600+ employees can easily be using data science to uncover useful insights.

My day to day job involves working with the business to tease out opportunities and prioritize them in a wider workforce context to develop interventions to improve. Due to the complexity of the problems, I will need to pick variables that make sense against traditional HR systems and not so traditional with around 8-14 variables that are important in the final analysis. When working on creating the right interventions it is important to have a model that you can easily explain. Model accuracy comes second and depending on the scenario optimizing for false positives may be just as important.

Most Important Asset

You need to gain the trust of senior leaders, you need to have an output that these leaders can consume and track over time. If you can strike a balance between explainability and accuracy then you can get buy-in on policies and strategies that will impact their most important asset, their workforce.

My tips for getting started in this space; try to beg, borrow and steal. Other departments may already be on this track so why not utilize their expertise in conducting an experiment or using a portion of their data warehouse? Having your own data warehouse will be important as you will often be dealing with 10-20 systems of input each having their own unique key such as employee id, email address, case number, card number etc.

Maintaining this data is difficult which is why it is essential to have processes to automate extract-transform-load (ETL). I use both R and Python with windows task scheduler all free to use, to perform these tasks and it has enabled members of my team to move away from data crunching and into data analysis and engagement.

Once you have a pipeline of data, you can then start to service your HR professional and people leaders with on-time insights, ideally as a consultancy model as you don't want to get stuck reproducing the same metric report with little to no value, what you do want is the ability to hold leaders to account on critical workforce issues and if intervention is having the right impact.

ANDREW PAUL ACOSTA

Data Scientist at Milesius Capital Resources

"Acquire domain knowledge, to be an effective data scientist in the particular field of your choice."

Path to Data Scientist

I lecture in different universities on finance and IT at a graduate level. My day job is doing data science, in support of capital markets. The line of work focuses on predictive analytics for credit firms, banks, assurance companies, and so on. I have been doing this for about eighteen years now. It is becoming increasingly difficult because data sets are getting larger and larger.

Crude Oil Trading and Potential Market Manipulation

My favorite data science project was looking at manipulation in the crude oil trading market. This was back in 2008, and I was working with a major petrochemical firm when the price of oil went up, and the price per barrel was about 148 USD. It looked like market manipulation, where the traders were just pushing up the price. My role was to look at it and examine the data, not just to look at price, but look at open interest. Open interest is how many future items had been sold, had been bought, and by the same buyer. Then we break that down by retail traders and commercial traders. Commercial traders are buyers and sellers. They want oil to be cheap as possible, because they have to benefit off turnovers from sales made.

During the refinery process, they crack oil into the different types of fuels. What I did was to look at who was actually shopping under these trades. I was also doing a series of analyses such as Granger Causality, looking at prices and observing the calculation driving the prices up, and so on. Who is piling on open interests? Who is buying contracts? And there are some things that are available on the Commodity Futures Trading Commission (CFTC).

I used to have very detailed reports every week. By breaking up commercial and noncommercial traders, it became easier to figure out who actually is doing what. It took me a couple of weeks to figure that out

When crude oil is traded, the trade is denominated in US dollars; and so is gold. No one was complaining when the price of gold was soaring, but they were complaining when the price of oil was getting too high. Upon some analysis, we figured that since both crude oil and gold were traded in USD, there might be something to look into there.

In the beginning, what looked like a crude oil issue became a USD strength issue. It took a few simulations, it took some testing, it took some regression analysis to look at it. When we looked at the price of crude oil and compared it to the price of gold (opposed to compare with USD), there seemed to be very little unusual behavior.

Why Gold Prices Mattered

I think well, a lot of it was just, curiosity. To look at different trends in trading, I think it requires certain domain knowledge. We see that oil prices are rising. Let's question what else is rising. By the way, look at gold, it's going through the roof. Then I thought, those two share something in common: they are both USD denominated. The next step was to use multivariable analysis, where you're looking at more than one variable, and see how that one affects the other.

I was looking at about ten years' worth of data, assessing the daily prices for crude, gold, US dollar, and so on. The tough part to figure out was, which factor was causing the other one to move. So, for an example, if the price of oil affects the dollar strength, dollar strength will affect the price of oil; and that's where the concept of Granger Causality comes in. When I teach this in my lecture, the example I give is—how do I know it's raining? Well, two hundred umbrellas are open. I know it's raining, but it doesn't make sense to think that if you're going to open the umbrella, there's going to be rain. It is clear that people open the umbrella because it's raining. With the USD, gold, and crude oil, it is not as easy to understand the causation.

Computers Will Take Over

The role of a data scientist will definitely be more self-oriented, but at some point computers will replace radiologists and other doctors given enough data to match relevant information on health.

Domain Knowledge Is Key

Strive to understand how a data set is put together. Then once you figure that out, move on to another one. The second thing is to keep updated, on current technologies, languages and so on. You don't necessarily have to know R, or Python, or so on, but learn about other languages. It's just sort of natural curiosity. Don't be satisfied once the answer is found; dig deeper as there could be more to uncover.

Acquire domain knowledge, to be an effective data scientist in the particular field of your choice. Look at different areas and learn a few things. Do a lot of general reading, and find out what's happening in regulations, or innovation in medicine, and so on.

ROSARIA SILIPO

PRINCIPAL DATA SCIENTIST AT KNIME

"Several students that graduate from university; they know how to use possible techniques but they don't know how to apply them in the real-world."

Types of Data Scientists

There are two kinds of data scientists: (1) the kind of data scientists that the companies want and (2) the kind of data scientists that actually exist.

Companies want someone who is proficient in machine learning, statistics, big data, traditional database and data storage platforms; basically, great at everything. In practice, this is rarely possible, so usually you have people who either grew up in machine learning, and then on the side they develop some kind of a skill.

On the opposite end, you have people who came out of the big data world and since they are dealing constantly with data they decided to learn something about machine learning. So usually their primary focus is on one of the two areas.

This is what happens in reality; then you have people who were programmers and then decided to recycle themselves as data scientists.

I think that the important thing is that you are open to learning new stuff constantly; it's a new area and nobody knows everything, so I guess your humility in not knowing and trying to learn more and more, is necessary.

Good Projects Makes You Think

I enjoyed all my projects but the ones that I liked the most were the ones where I needed to think a bit differently; I needed to add a twist to make it work.

Usually, you have some data and the customer requests. Then you have a set of algorithms and techniques and stuff that you can apply to reach the goal. Sometimes it's straightforward. You start with the data, apply machine learning, get some errors, minimize the errors, and then you get the result.

Anomaly Detection

Sometimes, it's a bit more complicated. For example, I had a project about anomaly detection and this one was a bit strange because they had data but in the data, they had no examples about the failure of the system. Without examples, you cannot really train any machine-learning algorithms.

We needed to think a bit differently. We trained the system on the normal data and then calculated the difference between the predicted data and the system data. If the difference was small enough, then you know everything was acting in normal conditions. Then if the difference was becoming bigger and the difference was lasting for a sufficiently long window of time, then you would set a trigger and conclude that, although you don't know what it is, something is not working in the normal condition.

It could be nothing, it could be something absolutely not important, but it could also be something really important.

Managing Unrealistic Expectations

It is really hard to manage the unrealistic expectations of customers. Sometimes they come to you, they give you zero data and they would like you to predict the next world crisis.

We can't create miracles; we cannot make data. I cannot give them something back if the data is not worth it. If its garbage, then I give them garbage.

Be Creative

The part that I like the most is when I have enough data and then I have to find some creative solution to get some nice results, then present them, and show them the nice things that you can actually do with data analysis. Sometimes it's really rewarding because you give them the results, and they are completely surprised; they are so happy.

Data Scientists Won't Go Away

The techniques are still evolving and we haven't reached the full maturity of the technology, so I think we have some years to go in the status quo as we are now. There is going to be more self-automated robots, self-learning, self-programming.

When machine learning was introduced, statisticians were worried that their jobs were going to disappear. That is not true because you still need to apply the machine learning; it's a different context and you need to learn it but probably there is going to be space for some of us again. I think it is going to become easier because what now is very complicated is also due to the immaturity of the technology.

Be Open Minded

Keep an open mind even if you think you know everything, because in this field we are always learning; it's never enough. Having a technical background is important but I would say that the best part is to keep an open mind on everything that is happening and learn as much as possible. Several students graduate from university; they know how to use all possible techniques but they don't know how to apply them in the real-world.

BEN TAYLOR

DATA SCIENTIST AT HIREVUE

"The biggest thing that stands out to me when I'm hiring for a data scientist is intrinsic motivation."

Path to Data Scientist

My background is like most data scientists who have been in the industry for a while; I did not study data science because they didn't have such a thing. I got my master's in chemical engineering and the entire time, all through my undergrad, graduate school and even through my work, I was very intense when it came to programming; especially for chemical engineering.

I've been using machine learning for thirteen years now, for different applications before data statistics became a big thing with widespread applications. The many turning points for me came when coworkers of mine told me about an opening where the hedge fund needed an artificial intelligence expert, who was also proficient in GPU computing and both those were things that I had been very passionate about on the side like hobbies. I was already doing GPU computing for fun, so I went and worked for this hedge fund.

After working at the hedge fund, I went back and worked for IM Flash Technologies. After about a year, I decided that the income difference between senior data scientist and senior chemical engineers was significant, and I wasn't happy there. I could make 50 percent more pay if I got a job as a data scientist compared to working as a chemical engineer. I wanted to work somewhere I was challenged, and at the time I was surprised at how easy it was to get job offers. This was because I had real-time experience and actually implemented machine algorithms in production, and I am proficient in machine languages; that was a recipe to get a lot of job offers.

I got three written job offers and five in total. It seemed like it wasn't that hard because I just kept getting these job offers. I ended up settling on two that I was going to go with; then by chance I went with HireVue, and I am really happy I did.

I joined HireVue as their first data scientist. I've worked there for three years and since joining there, I've hired three data scientists.

Hiring Criteria

The biggest thing that stands out to me when I'm hiring a data scientist is intrinsic motivation. The thing that's a real turnoff for me in applicants is when they say they want the job because they think it pays great and the problems are interesting. I don't actually want to hire that person. I want to hire the person who is obsessed with it and they say, oh I did this sentiment analysis last week, I turned it into a little app, and the whole thing was a complete failure, and then the next week, I did this other thing.

That's something that stood out to me. I was speaking at a university about what data science specifically is, deep learning. I was going through the presentation, and I didn't know any of the students in the audience. One of the students in the front row kept asking questions. I could tell based on his questions that he was a sharp kid. He knew technical terms related to the languages, the libraries, and the methods. He'd actually been a passionate user for weeks if not months, and after meeting that individual briefly, even after leaving that meeting because they were all interested in getting a job. "How do I get jobs? How can I get jobs? I want to get a good job when I graduate." And I could tell after leaving that meeting that this individual, this kid in the front row whom I don't know, would have no problem getting a job. Sure enough—within three weeks, he landed a job at another company as their first data scientist; I heard he was up against PhD level applicants, and he was a master's dropout.

He got the job over the better-qualified applicants and I think the biggest difference is he obviously loves what he's doing and that shows in what he does.

The three data scientists we've hired all have PhDs, but I would have jumped at the chance to hire this kid just because he has such strong intrinsic motivation. He knew a lot of things that most of the applicants didn't know. That's because he's self-taught, he's self-motivated, and he's kind of diving in head first.

Removing Racism and Sexism—Machine Learning

My favorite to date has to do with deep learning; removing racism and sexism from a model with machine learning. I built a model that can make predictions that can actively remove bias, and so if you give me a really racist performance training set or sexist training set, I can still build and predict a model that will predict the performance that you wanted but remove the bias.

That was my first project to work on because you are fighting two different objectives. We didn't want to limit ourselves to just a specific modeling method. We want to be able to handle multiple modeling methods and at the end of doing that project be able to show that if you gave me a performance set that has so much bias and that was actually audit worthy, you would be legally on the chopping block based on this training set. We could remove that racism and get it within acceptable levels, but we could still have a model that predicted performance and offered value to the original customer.

Another interesting project was predicting human attractiveness using deep learning, and that was fun. Based on an image, the computer would predict how attractive a man or a woman was using deep learning.

They had the world's first artificial intelligence (AI) beauty contest, in which computers predicted how beautiful you were. They had an international competition to see who the most beautiful person was when someone noticed that the top fifty picks, both men and women, and from different age brackets were all white. There were no dark-skinned people, Hispanic people, or black people, and when I saw that, I was frustrated because people were not thinking about this when they should be. So I downloaded million images of men and women who had been rated, and I was able to build my own attractiveness classifier. My immediate reaction was that I wanted to do a blog post to jab at them a little bit to say "the first nonracist beauty contest" to show that I had actively fixed the thing that they should have fixed in the first place.

The other thing that was really interesting and that I was surprised about was that the data set was international, and it came from all these other countries, so racism was worldwide. Even in Africa, people were biased toward others with lighter skin. I heard people say this before; we just have this sad reality of humanity that we can do all this machine learning, but sometimes you can't fix the training set.

Don't Delay—Go for It!

I think one of the things I would tell them right away is don't delay. I would encourage everyone reading this book to do everything they can to become a data scientist as quickly as they can. So how can you get a job offer now, a month from now, two months from now? And it doesn't have to be the best job, just a job as a data scientist.

JOHN BOTTEGA

Senior Advisor—Chief Data Officer Forum

"The data scientist is going to be as good as
the quality of data that they acquire."

Data Cleaning Responsibilities

If we do data management right that means we are delivering data that is trusted and consistent. Unfortunately, this is rarely the case and consumers of the data spend more time cleansing it than in analyzing it.

The data scientist is in some senses no different from any end user. Every end user should be able to find the data. That's another issue. They keep spending huge amounts of time to track down necessary data.

We need to be able to trust the data and to aggregate the data. If you think about the financial crisis, it was really a result of the lack of ability to see the interconnectedness of data.

Several industries are suffering from this as well. Those who have actually done pretty well are in the medical research space. My son-in-law is a research scientist and he tells me that in his field, they need to be able to talk to others around the globe about discoveries in a common language.

Why Data?

I have always found information interesting. I was a programmer before and I loved it. I still wish I could go back and play—it was fun. When I went to Lehman Brothers in 1991, I took a role in data quality. I got into it—it was like a puzzle. I mean look at the data and see how all the pieces come together. There's a hidden meaning behind the pieces that if you put them in the right order exposes the answer to you. That's part of the attraction

End-User Support

It's kind of our responsibility as data practitioners to make sure that we support that end user. And enable them to do their job in the best way possible. You can't uncouple data scientists from the data practitioners. They tend to be coupled together because they are so dependent on each other. The data scientist is going to be as good as the quality of data that he or she acquires.

STEVEN TEDJAMULIA

CEO AT PREDICTIVE NETWORK

*"The cool part is when the data is clean and you find
results and it all comes together. It's like training
for a triathlon, the best part is the end."*

Career Path

I first started out with Dell computers, where I ran the visualization group and had several people working for me. At that point, I didn't think about how big predictive analytics could become, but I knew there was something there.

After running the group for a while, I decided to take a step back and do something smaller, so they gave me permission to lead a small group, and not report to anyone for a period of seven months. Whatever I would make I could pull back to the group, so I had my own P&L. It was fun to see how we went from $0 to $500,00 in revenue within a few months. I was hiring people to work for me as contractors to grow it and eventually bought the predictive science group from Dell.

My passion is to really help people; it's something I always wanted to do. To that end, I started Predictive Network. This is where my passion to help data scientists came from. There are several initiatives that we have underway, such as the data science help desk and a recruiting arm. I'm now in a position to give back and help others.

At this point we are over fifteen thousand data scientist members; more than a thousand people visit the website every day. We have a few advisory boards. We are also on track to pull off the largest online data science conference.

Commoditized Data Science

There is currently ample number of job opportunities in the data science space. Data science is becoming more commoditized. Cheaper technology, prices will fall, and open source will get bigger; dealing with easier and simpler tools. Optimization—people will consume more in less time. Function isn't going away; it's just being brought into the mainstream. We are driving at efficiency right now. Some companies have cool technology but aren't sure how to get the data scientists to use it.

If you are a data scientist, learning R and Python become very important as data science merges more and more with computer science. To get paid more, you'd need to learn the technologies. There are some jobs that will get offshored, which will lessen the need for some skills (e.g., data cleaning and other trivial tasks).

Customer Conversion Uplift

This project had the highest return at Dell. We took the list of all customers of Dell (from the CRM), took the social data from our communities, looked at products they purchased, and looked at IP addresses to see which customer would buy what product next and who the salesperson should contact. The results were fantastic; we had about 20 percent uplift in new leads and 50 percent uplift in conversion.

This was before all these new tools came out. I used R, Python, Salesforce, and other databases to bring in data, pull it from the warehouse, integrate it with the business CRM, and build a user interface to it.

Data Wrangling and Results

Data wrangling is horrible; I usually stick in a movie in the background, or else I would fall asleep. I got a stationary bicycle under my desk to pass the time.

The cool part is when the data is clean and you find results and it all comes together. It's like training for a triathlon, the best part is the end. You spend most of the time training and preparing for it; but the best part is hitting your target time. In my career, I've watched a lot of movies and shed many pounds!

Have a Portfolio

I talk to data scientists every day, at all levels. I always ask people to tell me about themselves and what they do. The ones that kill it say here are the ten projects I did; here's my portfolio; here is my best practice sharing group; I participate in nonprofit and speak at these conferences. It shows leadership, portfolio of work, and so on. Ask the interviewer to give you a test to show your skills.

We try to give people speaking opportunities, help them engage on projects and create portfolios, and build people up to help them become senior data scientists or whatever they want to accomplish.

JARED P. LANDER

CHIEF DATA SCIENTIST LANDER ANALYTICS

*"Data cleaning is something you need to do before
the fun stuff. The fun stuff is not the main show.
Statistics is the most important thing I can do."*

Path to Data Scientist

In undergrad, I majored in mathematics by accident, and I wanted to major in business communications. I started taking math classes for fun. I took so many math classes that professors and my mother encouraged me to finish my degree in mathematics. I did it and was very happy about it. Once I finished college, I decided to get into the music industry to manage bands.

After a few years, I decided that this wasn't for me. I got a job in business intelligence, essentially building dashboards. The company specialized in the fashion industry and was a good step forward into a tech career. I was good in statistics, math, and data. I applied to graduate school, went to Columbia, got a master's, and happened to graduate during the financial crisis, when "data" was becoming a hot topic. This got me into the trend of data scientist and was very fortunate with the timing.

Motivation for "R for Everyone"

I got the initial motivation from someone asking me to write a book; R is fun and is my favorite tool to use.

The ability to spread knowledge so I can help other people learn to use R was really exciting. I wrote it from the point of view of how I would've wanted to learn it. I learned in in a very frustrating way. I wanted it to flow in a helpful way for those just starting out.

New York Open Statistical Programming Meetup

We are always fully booked but have space constraints (event venues can typically hold about 250 people). There's an increasing interest in data-related events. It's become so popular that membership has reached locations outside New York. We are also starting to live-stream the event so everyone can join.

Likes and Dislikes

I enjoy when I get to do modeling, statistics, and playing with R; however, the most important thing I do is the statistics and modeling and fortunately for me that stuff is also fun. Data cleaning is something you need to do before the fun stuff. The fun stuff is not the main show. Statistics is the most important thing I can do.

Cool Projects

While a few projects come to mind, it's a tie between my thesis—on what makes NYC pizzerias popular and a work project to help Minnesota Vikings do their draft picks. Pizza thing was fun because I'm obsessed with pizza. I got to do a cool project to use data to analyze pizza (using R). The Vikings are participating in a very popular sport in the country. There's also a lot riding on their draft picks. My models are affecting millions of dollars of decisions. It is literally just the draft weekend, not stretched over time. I also used R for this project as well as some databases to store the data. So far, I haven't come across anything R can't do.

I also create educational videos with Pearson and DataCamp.

Words of Wisdom

Learn statistics, the math, the science behind it all. Don't just learn tools; know the statistics. This will make you truly valuable.

Learn how to program; no matter which language you choose, you need to do your job programmatically.

Be able to communicate; be social and interactive, work within the community, and interact with everyone you can.

The data community is very open, and there are lots of opportunities. Join some meet-ups, talk to people, go on Twitter, interact with people, make friends, and learn from each other. Meet-ups are referred to as the best night school you can go to. The real meet-up is the bar after the meet-up. This means spending time talking to people and contributing back to the community.

DAVID RUBAL

Chief Technologist, Data and Analytics
Principal Data Scientist at DLT

"Build a solid foundation of knowledge and experience,
be disruptive and be a continuous learner. "

Path to Data Scientist

I 've been building my career focused on data. My career base was telecommunications and infrastructure. I worked with some early players of data and Internet technology. This really helped build my data skills set and my data knowledge-base from the ground up from the network up to compute, and now more specialized data-centric areas, like cybersecurity, Internet of Things, and so on.

I've been involved in big data and data science for the last ten years—from a theoretical and practical, hands-on perspective.

Never Stop Learning

Today, the profile to what it takes to be successful is to keep evolving—continuous learning as well as tactical experience. What I do today as a CTO and active and practicing data scientist is because I kept learning; it's a field that's evolving rapidly. I always held other roles that helped me build my business and communication skills.

It's not only about being able to gather data, research data, manipulate data, visualize data; it's also about the outcome. This equates to capabilities, improved situations, basically ensuring the right outcome.

Having a good base in statistics, data analytics (from wrangling, exploration to visualizing and story-telling) is crucial. It's important to be able to leverage data, be able to shape and tell the story behind data. That's what you hear—that a lot in people focus maybe just on the analytics and visualization type because we are visual; people are visual. We need to see things. Sometimes it helps to tell that story, where data can support it. It's all about being able to look at all factors together and shape that into an effective story and effective outcome.

There's a lot of education associated with this role, helping the business become more data savvy. It used to be that only IT folks cared about understanding data; today, almost everyone needs to be empowered to understand data.

Data for Good

I'm a big believer of data for good. Leveraging data to improve our society, leverage open data on all levels to help us work with each other, be part of a data-driven team.

I'm also particularly impressed in the early work that's been done around leveraging data from a health care perspective and being able to provide as much impact to determine where patterns are in societies and across the world—to elevate and provide better care.

To me all the data is good, and the data social efforts underway are also welcome. They're all tagged with the same challenge: taking on society's problems and being able to leverage a combination of private data and open data, scraping data wherever they can find it to be able to take some of these challenges. So I really commend these organizations for being able to take on something like this and keep the conversations on, keep that work on, keep support.

The evolution of blockchain technologies is one of the key factors of how we will manage and use data going forward in, for example, health care, finance, and government. When you start to integrate use of blockchain, the relationship that you have with your private information will help you determine in the blockchain model who has access to the data. This will allow data to be more efficiently used and to be more secure.

Words of Advice

Build a solid foundation of knowledge and experience, be disruptive, and be a continuous learner. This space is rapidly evolving, as we've discussed here, in so many different ways and whether you're a formal data scientist with a title and role or you're just passionate about data science and the use of data to be able to get to an insightful outcome, it's really exciting. Continue to challenge the traditional models, the current state of thinking, and the current state of technology.

It's an area where people will be able to find ways of growing personally, professionally, and in their communities in ways that they may have not even considered and in taking that knowledge and spreading it. Be an advocate for data science at all levels of life. Help people become comfortable working with data and using data and telling the story behind data. All that isn't possible until you actually engage in working with data science and in every aspect of it; that is my guidance.

RENEE M. P. TEATE

DATA SCIENTIST AT HELIOCAMPUS

"Learning data science is not a quick process, and there will be times when a challenge feels too difficult, but you will overcome challenges or reroute around them, and before you know it, you will have marketable skills and be working as a data scientist!"

Becoming a Data Scientist

I started my *Becoming a Data Scientist* blog first, because I was in a machine-learning class in grad school, where I was getting a master's in systems engineering. On top of the course being difficult, I was also teaching myself Python so I could do the exercises in a language I wanted to learn, and I wanted to track my progress so I wouldn't forget what I had learned in the fast-moving course, so that's how the blog originated.

Then, in the summer of 2015, just after I finished my master's program, I was ready to dive into some more in-depth data science projects and was watching others do the same, so I started the hashtag #SoDS, for Summer of Data Science, on Twitter so it could be a group learning experience. It was fun, and many other people joined in the hashtag, and we were sharing tutorials and learning experiences, and I started to gain a following. I also started to build DataSciGuide, a data science learning directory where people review learning resources and their reviews are tied to their experience level, during that summer.

In my last semester of grad school, winter/spring of 2015, I had to drive about an hour to class twice a week (my program had been primarily online, but they weren't offering a course I needed to graduate, so I decided to make the commute), and I had started listening to a lot of data science podcasts so I could spend those hours learning. So many of the data science interviews fascinated me, but they were all focused on what the data scientists were doing now.

I was left with questions: "How did these awesome people get to where they are professionally? What are their backgrounds? What does it really take to become a data scientist?" I also wanted to hear from a wider variety of data scientists, so I had the idea to start a podcast about becoming a data scientist myself. I have a habit of coming up with crazy ideas, not knowing whether or not they're possible, and giving them a try. Sometimes that doesn't end well, but in this case, I guess the topic resonated with others, because I started gaining listeners and Twitter followers quickly as soon as I published the first episode, even though the audio and video quality wasn't great! I really didn't know what I was doing, and I admit that I still have issues with recording the podcasts fifteen episodes in, but I enjoy the interviews enough to keep going.

I was really excited that the *Becoming a Data Scientist* podcast had taken off, and by the end of "Season 1" (when I took a break from recording while I started new job in July 2016), I was getting over two thousand listeners per episode and had almost ten thousand followers on Twitter. Those numbers have been growing since!

Good Data Scientist

The critical technical skill sets are covered often, but I think people often think you need to be a lot more advanced than you do to get started in the field professionally. You definitely need a solid understanding of basic descriptive statistics and data visualization techniques, the ability to code in a language such as R or Python to manipulate and summarize large data sets, and enough knowledge of machine learning to properly apply packages such as the scikit-learn Python machine-learning package. You also need a good understanding of model evaluation techniques, so you know whether the model you built was a good one, or if it needs work, be able to dive in and problem-solve. With these basics, you can work with data programmatically, run data sets through already-vetted algorithms, and understand the results.

You don't need to be an expert in these things in order to start applying for jobs—just have the experience of going through the model development and improvement cycle using real-world data sets several times, and understanding what you can and can't conclude based on those models. Once you have the basics down, you can go further in particular "elective" areas, such as natural language processing, computer vision, big data engineering, and data visualization for publication. A willingness to continue learning on the job is obviously important, but there are so many companies looking for data professionals, you might be valuable to one of them long before you convince yourself you are marketable.

Beyond the technical skills, an ability to communicate in the domain in which you want to work is critical. You need a grasp of the terminology and concepts of the domain you want to work in—whether it's an area of scientific research, business, education, or other area—you can't just churn through the numbers and give a statistical readout. You need to be able to listen and understand a problem described in nontechnical terms, translate that into a question that data can answer, do the actual analysis, and then translate that back into the language of the domain, so your results are intelligible to someone who doesn't "speak data." A common complaint among managers trying to hire data scientists is that many have great technical skills but don't know how to talk to people who aren't data scientists, which is vital if their analysis is to be used by less-technical colleagues to make decisions.

Curiosity and creativity are also important in data science. The ability to ask follow-up questions and dig deeper into the data to answer questions that surround the question you were originally tasked to answer is a great trait. Many of the data scientists I have interviewed on my podcast have singled out a curiosity about how things work as something that has driven them to become a good data scientist, or a something that sets data science candidates apart.

Future of Data Science

I think there will be more formal training programs available for data scientists (data science master's degrees are already popping up around the country as higher education institutions adjust to the market), and I hope there will be more courses on ethics and bias in machine learning and other topics that don't necessarily involve learning math or code but are still important for data scientists to understand, since our work can be so impactful to people's lives.

Proud Moments

I'm proud of my constant growth throughout my career, and have realized that "lifelong learning" is a common (and, one can argue, necessary) trait among data scientists. I have tried to keep expanding my skills and didn't officially become a data scientist until I was thirty-four years old.

I am also really proud of my role as a data science online community leader because of my *Becoming a Data Scientist* podcast, creation of the Data Science Learning Club and DataSciGuide, and growing Twitter following. I know that it isn't easy to become a data scientist, but that with enough effort, people from a wide variety of career and educational backgrounds can enjoy this exciting career path, so I try to provide resources and encourage people who are interested in this field. Anyway, it's more fun to do something when you have a bunch of friends along for the ride, right?

Favorite Project

I have a variety of favorites, but I would say that my role in building a database and interface for storing and exploring the outcomes of predictive analytics projects at HelioCampus is my favorite right now! Maybe my latest project is always my favorite!

For this project, I have combined a variety of tools and techniques I have learned over the years. With help from my colleagues, I designed a relational database using SQL to store information about each model, a summary of the results each time the predictions are run, and the prediction details. I used Python and scikit-learn to develop the machine-learning algorithms that are generating the predictions, and I am building dashboards in Tableau to enable end users to visually compare models, explore the model parameters, features, and predictions, and to better understand how the results change over time as more and different data becomes available to the algorithm.

HelioCampus is an analytics company that works with universities and higher ed institutions, and I'm excited that the results of this project will be put to use at schools to help administrators make decisions so they can provide better services to their students.

I wouldn't say I have run into any big obstacles, necessarily. But then again, I tend to see obstacles as interesting challenges that are part of the process. For instance, even though we are just starting out with implementing this project, we have to keep in mind a variety of possible future uses of the system and design for those. I think it's fun to brainstorm all the different types of information we might want to store in this system in the future, and attempt to design it to be able to handle those future applications. This requires some rework as we realize limitations we might be building in, but that is a part of the design process.

Words of Wisdom
Since most data science students today are using online resources to teach themselves, I think a good thing to keep in mind is that only you can keep yourself from getting derailed. This isn't like school where everyone has to move through the topic at the teacher's pace: you can

go as slow or as fast as you're comfortable with, and reach out to a variety of resources along the way.

Some people might make comments that discourage you, or you might get really stuck on a project, and it's up to you not to give up in the face of challenges. Go to meet-ups and conferences to generate ideas, but don't get overwhelmed by the huge variety of topics under the "umbrella" of data science; you don't have to learn them all! Focus on learning the core basics that all data scientists need: basic statistics, programming in a language like Python or R, and applying machine-learning packages and understanding the results. From there, you can delve into more advanced versions of the basic topics, and choose your favorite "sub-topic" of data science as your specialty.

Learning data science is not a quick process, and there will be times when a challenge feels too difficult, but you will overcome challenges or reroute around them, and before you know it, you will have marketable skills and be working as a data scientist!

JUNE ANDREWS

PRINCIPAL DATA SCIENTIST

"People who want to excel early in their data science career, I think must align their abilities to answer tough questions with an eco-system level understanding of what generates value to the business and the users."

Favorite Project

One project I'll always remember working on was at LinkedIn. At the time, there was quite a bit of press around how successful women were less liked than successful men. The root of the press was from the Heidi Roizen study in which Columbia Business School students were presented with two identical resumes, one from Heidi and one from Howard. While, both Heidi and Howard had equal competencies, Howard was perceived as likable, while Heidi was deemed selfish. I thought there was more to the story, I didn't believe that was the complete picture. Coincidentally, I was working at LinkedIn, arguably the best data source to get a wide reaching, cross industry, cross company, cross gender in-depth perspective to profile the careers of successful men and women. For this particular question, we had endorsements and executives. We had who had endorsed, who for what skills at what time, and who was an executive. All told, we had millions of companies, executives, and endorsements.

The results were gorgeous - there was more to the story. Once you took at step back and looked at all of the data a more complete picture emerged. Yes, for large companies men were more liked than women.

But, executives at large companies were less well liked than executives at small companies. In fact, women in executive roles at small companies were the most well liked of all executives! So the story wasn't that if you wanted to be well liked take inspiration for successful men, the complete picture was if you wanted to be well liked take inspiration from women leading small companies.

That paradigm shift of understanding from taking all of the data into account has stuck with me throughout my career. I prioritize understanding the eco-system and taking a holistic view to evaluating the impact of data science projects.

Tools and Approach

My philosophy on data science tools is to use what is available and works. In general the set of tools you'll need is a pipeline starting with one of many SQL-like languages, piping data into a Turing complete language like Python or R, a visualization package like D3 or RStudio, and a communication platform like a wiki or a slide deck. My advice is to learn one tool for each layer of the stack and then adopt new tools and languages on an as needed based. For this particular project at LinkedIn the supported stack was Pig+Python, R, D3, and Power Point.

The approach was slow, then fast and finally rigorous. The start only involved research and literature reviews. I didn't touch the data for a full month. I primarily worked on other projects and communicated with psychologists on how these types of studies were conducted and what parallels they saw with how people used LinkedIn. Then I touched the data. I knew the data well and leveraged many previous scripts. Analyzing the data took days and quickly lead to the conclusions shared. Finally, the conclusions had to be rigorously tested. How the data was handled at every critical stage leading to the conclusion was peer reviewed and when appropriate re-tested.

What do you think makes a good data scientist?

People who want to excel early in their data science career, I think must align their abilities to answer tough questions with an eco-system level understanding of what generates value to the business and the users.

What are the upsides and downsides of data science?

For some people, I think data science latches on to an element of their personality they couldn't fully utilize any other way. In my free time, I've made a hobby out of turning buying a car and purchasing a home into a data-driven decision. When it came to gardening, I modeled how climate change is affecting tulips across the US to see if I needed to adjust my landscaping. The limits you hit for hobby data science projects, between the availability of data and impact of your work, are brutally frustrating. Then I go to work, at a company that has removed the data limits and for whom which, only large impact will do. This is an incredible upside.

The downsides naturally follow from the upside. High impact data science roles are inherently high stress roles. One reason is you have to work across the board, not just play to your strengths. If you're great at data story-telling, you still have to do rigorous research. If you're great at modeling you still have to communicate. It's not enough to understand the answer - it's not enough to be right. You have to go out and convince other people that you're right, and help them adjust their actions accordingly.

The impact data scientists make with their work can change lives. Once you get past your first year as a data scientist and start to be trusted with bigger decisions, you'll probably experience more stress. I recommend investing in stress management techniques early in your career.

Changing Role of Data Scientists

We can generally predict five years out, pretty well. The primary trend I'm seeing, is a shift from isolated data scientists to an increase in the number of data science teams. With teams, you can allocate people according to their strengths. An individual no longer operates across the full stack from logging data to sharing conclusions, but becomes specialized in a few areas. Accordingly, we're seeing an increase in Data Engineering, Data Analytics and Machine Learning Engineering roles.

Originally, the duties of those roles were included in a Data Science role. As the roles become increasingly specialized and the breadth of skill requirements lessen, the time to close an open role will shorten. Companies won't have to wait months for a unicorn data scientist to come along. Accordingly, as fewer skills are required salaries will adjust.

The other major trend is the rapid increase in degrees from universities and the number of graduates. With this centralization of how data scientists are trained, I believe the field will develop a formalization of what it means to be a data scientist and solidify the methodologies for data science to systematically innovate.

In ten years, there will be a broader reach of data science skills and philosophies into all industries. Eventually, I hope a data science course will become as common place a requirement as a course in mathematics is to complete any STEM degree.

Robots Taking Data Science Jobs?

While we've seen increased automation of what used to be part of a data scientist's job, including cleaning data, visualization, even anomaly detection, I don't think successful data scientists will ever go jobless. Successful data scientists make a job for themselves wherever they go, by creating value. They are inherently creative and exploratory people. If we automate the entire data platform, you will see more realistic expectations on how many data scientists companies need. Across the fields, while I think the total number of data scientists needed for specific tasks may go down, the total number of data scientists will increase due to demand across industries.

Words of Wisdom

The most common career question I'm asked is whether or not to do a boot camp. I'm old school; I grew up on a farm and have an inherent bias toward "if you can get paid to do the job you want to do, then go get paid to do that job." If you can get hired directly into a data science role, go forth and conquer. Often times, people don't realize how viable an option that is, and they take it off the table before choosing. You may even be able to become a data scientist in your current company. Think of how to start your career as your first data science project, you'll find many options.

Data science is a field that has to and has grown as a community. Most early data scientists started in small companies and isolated teams, spread across industries. The wealth of knowledge in the field has come from these data scientists collaborating, sharing learnings at conferences, in books, blogs, open source, teaching and coaching each other. Personally, where appropriate I publish my work and philosophies on what data science can do to help contribute to the community. In receiving feedback and learning from other folks, it helps me stay current with the field and expand my abilities as a data scientist.

Once you work through a few data science problems, take a moment. Pause and think about what you have to contribute. I'll bet it's an idea worth sharing.

ARMANDO VIEIRA

DATA SCIENTIST AT CONTEXTVISION AB

"There must be a vision to put data science side by side to the CEO or CFO depending on the size of organization to empower data scientists and transform the culture of the company."

Path to Data Scientist

I started data science soon after my PhD in 1997. I realized that physics was not an easy field to make a breakthrough. So as chances of getting the Nobel Prize were slim, I thought of jumping into other areas that are newer and attracted my attention. One such area was neural networks. I began working with neural networks in physics and got good results. I spent ten years in academia and later worked as a consultant on projects.

Favorite Project

One project that I really liked was for a company called Certify Medical. It was very interesting because it was a really hard problem and involved messy data. There are several molecules, proteins, and genes, and you have to come up with a hypothesis to help pharmaceutical industries to find new drugs for diseases.

You have to somehow reverse engineer all the biological engineering, which is rather complex. We also had text based on machine readings of medical journal to extract information. The analysis process in biology is difficult and complex due to causality; it is hard to infer what is causing what.

It was a project I liked working on a lot. It combined graphical databases using deep learning for normal representation and also some visualization based on that.

Future of Data Science

The data science role will be key and pivotal in organizations. Transformation needs to take place for organizations to stop putting data scientists into the IT department. Data science is not in the IT department; this is what I keep repeating all the time. There must be a vision to put data science side by side to the CEO or CFO depending on the size of the organization to empower data scientists and to transform the culture of the company.

It's really important and I think data scientists should have more power. It's difficult because most data scientists are technical and may not have the expertise in project management, marketing, business, and so on.

Opportunities in the Future

Customer Service—I see big potential to impact customer service with data science. Machines can read texts, understand voice, can reply in voice, and so on. Everything that can be automated will be automated.

Marketing—Several pieces of marketing can be automated. Machine can read and understand millions of data points; this is something humans are just not able to execute; it's just impossible for the human brain to analyze such great amounts of data.

People fear machines and algorithms taking over their jobs; they feel threatened by data science. It's a power struggle. Some automation needs to be done; there is so much space for improvement.

Blockchain—This will be a game changer; it will enable trust to be built and will also allow the building of new business models and products with enhanced transparency and security. I'm actually reading a really interesting book right now called *The Business Block Chain*, by William Mougayar. It's a good book.

I believe it's really a game-changing technology to create new opportunity for decentralization. You don't basically replace all central organizations like central banks, public services, and replace them with peer-to-peer mechanism built on trust. It's just a smarter way to do it. Yes! I think it's very powerful.

Words of Advice

I think you should get your hands dirty. Start with simple projects. There are plenty of things on the Internet (such as Kaggle competitions). Pick the one you like the most, and go with it. Learn how to code using R and Python, which are common languages.

I don't suggest you start with deep learning initially; it's very cool and may look simple, but there are a lot of tricks in it. Just start with simple stuff, such as regression, and random forests, and so on. Start playing with your data. Start asking questions, and start visualizing data. Think what you can do with it; mix different data sets together.

The best way to learn is to practice and, as soon as possible, get into real data problems.

People say that algorithms are the hardest part of data science. I disagree. The hard part is understanding the problem, framing the problem for data science, and adapting the tools you have to solve the problem. That is the hard part.

The value you can add is to determine how you can save your company money, create new profits, reformulate the process to make it more efficient, and so on. It is really important to learn to communicate effectively, to educate the business not to be threatened by data science, and to see it as a tool to empower the business.

This is something you can't learn from books as all businesses are different; you must learn by doing.

CHARLES GIVRE

SENIOR LEAD DATA SCIENTIST—STRATEGIC INNOVATION GROUP AT BOOZ ALLEN HAMILTON

"I would say that if someone is serious about it, then dive into it, start learning things and find a project to work on."

From Music Major to Data Scientist

I definitely had an unusual career path. I was originally a music major in undergrad and kind of decided that I really didn't want to do that on a full-time basis. At the time, the Internet was taking off; I was really interested in building websites—not just consumer-based websites but stuff like Amazon. I figured that computer science would be a good way to go.

As I neared graduation, I realized that it was not the right career for me, but I was too far into it at that point of time, and knew I should just finish it. But by the end of it, a number of things happened. One was that 9/11 happened. At that time, I basically had only one more class to graduate and had a year of scholarship left.

I decided to take a class I was interested in. I took a Middle Eastern history class and absolutely loved it. I decided to study Middle Eastern politics and history. I wasn't sure where I was going with that, but I continued on. I was thinking that I wanted to be a professor. Therefore, after my master's, I looked into PhD programs.

I was also always doing tech stuff all the time. So that was more like a side job, such as building websites and doing tech stuff for companies.

What ended up happening was the CIA team had job openings, and I interviewed, thinking that I would never get a job there.

I submitted an application, and they invited me for an interview. I thought I'd go, but there was no way I'd be hired.

I actually got an offer and ended up working there for five years. I did a lot of analytic work. What I really gained from the agency was that when I started there, they put me through very rigorous programs to teach analytics. This involved a lot of critical thinking, how to write effectively, how to give presentations effectively, and so on. It's been enormously valuable in things that I have done.

From what I have seen, I feel that they don't teach critical thinking very well in school these days. I also am not a fan of the way schools are teaching basic writing and communication skills. Along with critical thinking skills, it is important to be able to communicate and write effectively.

I had a great time working there, but the commute was awful, and I was really getting burned out. I decided to look for work closer to home. So I started applying and got a job at Booz Allen.

My first job at this new company was kind of tedious. It basically involved moving a lot of data around on spreadsheets. The agency I worked for had Python available to you on the computer. I started tinkering with it and automating everything I was doing. This led me to building dashboards. Then I started building prototypes around analytics that could do things faster than a person could do it.

So this was how I got into what people now call data science.

Good Data Scientist

There's a Venn diagram floating out there on the Internet, and I see that as the bare minimum. You need to have some combination of those skills (hacking skills, math & statistics knowledge, and substitutive expertise).

On top of that, you need to have an insatiable curiosity and solid critical thinking skills. You should also know things such as various technology types, beyond Python and R, and understand how systems work together.

Additionally, a good understanding of the subject matter you are working on is really important. People tend to overlook this. You can't expect a math expert to just know what to do in various situations. I have a quick story about this specific point. There was a data scientist who was analyzing the characters of a video game, and after spending a long time on her analysis, she concluded that there was one character in the game that was able to complete the entire game in half the time as others. Upon this finding, she was told that this was how the game was developed on purpose. This is what I mean about understanding the subject matter.

Hiring Data Scientists

I look for the critical thinking component: how to pick apart a problem and get to the key steps and approach to solving the problem. During an interview, I try to ask a question that is somewhat realistic but doesn't have an obvious answer. I ask simple questions and get more complex as the questions continue. I present a real problem and see how they approach it.

Technical Skills vs. Domain Expertise

The approach to becoming a domain expert is good. It is harder to acquire than data science skills. There are so many courses and books on machine learning and coding. It is more difficult to absorb the knowledge of the intracranial of an industry or environment. Obviously, it's even easier if the domain experts have some basic technological skills.

Machine Learning and Car Data

A project that I worked on last year was a research project. I was analyzing the data that was gathered from cars and applying machine learning to that. My initial goal was to see what we could learn about an individual from the data that that individual's car is gathering about him or her.

I started playing with it and figuring out patterns, such as driving behavior and other things that probably won't surprise you. I wanted to see if I could identify the driver based on the data I gathered. I looked at things such as whether people stepped on the brake really hard and other nuances of driving. I did a lot of experiments and was able to build a model that works pretty well.

I see enormous use for this model. There's a potential for new security analytics. For authentication, there's a paradigm for approving people; we can check things like what you have (token), what you know (password), or what you are (biometric). A possible fourth way to authenticate is what you do. How cool would it be if your car can understand that it's not you driving the car and alert authorities or alert you of that? It definitely has a lot of potential.

Approach

I have a Bluetooth collection device in a vehicle; it collects data and puts it into spreadsheet. Then I use Python to analyze and visualize the data. I tend to use Python more than others. There are several libraries available for getting and preparing data for the type of work that I do. I think R does analytics a bit better, but Python is catching up to that. Choice of languages isn't as important; picking one and getting good at it is my advice. Then if you need to learn another one, you can pick it up easily.

Words of Advice

It's a great time to be in this field because there are so many opportunities and resources available, in terms of online videos, conferences, all these kinds of things. I would say that if someone is serious about it, then dive into it, start learning things, and find a project to work on. Don't worry about whether you are a data scientist or not; don't worry about that. Just start diving into things and experimenting in areas like groups. Start doing things that people talk about, start talking to them, and do that kind of thing. Just get in and go for it. Find the area where you want to apply data science—something like health care or security, and so on. Don't forget about developing business expertise and the end goal of creating value.

Bonus Section

If you decide that data science is the career for you, continue reading for some tips on interviewing for open job opportunities.

Interview Tips

Although the demand for data science is high, people still need to demonstrate the appropriate skills in order to land a job in the field. In this section, we'll discuss some interview tips and sample questions and answers. The key thing is to show your passion for the area and be yourself. It is helpful if you have relevant projects to discuss and a project portfolio to point to.

The best way to prepare for an interview is to read the job description very carefully and understand the requirements of the role. See if you can relate an example to each of the components of the roles and be comfortable citing a specific example when you executed similar tasks or showed similar competencies or skills. If you don't have the relevant experience, you can work on sample projects to build your knowledge.

Additionally, do some research on the industry that the company represents. Understand the pain points of that industry, and be able to speak intelligently about key trends and challenges.

Interview questions

- **What type of experience do you have with programming languages?** Do you have knowledge of R or Python? What is your proficiency level? How did you end up learning this? Talk about courses you took, internships undertaken, and on-the-job learning.
- **What are your strengths?** Are you great at solving complex data problems? Are you the best at communicating with executives? Do you have a deep knowledge or expertise with a specific software or tool? Draw attention to and accentuate your overall strengths.
- **What are your weaknesses?** This is a difficult one...in this case I always encourage an honest and candid response. For example, there was a role I applied for that required knowledge of four different systems. I was highly proficient at one of the four systems (Salesforce); however, I had never used the other three systems. When asked about my weakness I told the recruiter that

my weakness would be getting up to speed with the other three systems I had never worked with before. Be ready to discuss this question.

- **Why are you interested in working for [insert company name here]?** This is a common question—they want to see that you are not just applying to every company that has a job opening. Read their mission and vision, and see if that is something you can point to when answering this question.

- **Are you willing to relocate?** This is an important question that you need to plan ahead to have an answer for. Job descriptions tend to have the preferred location, so you would be able to see if this is a requirement.

- **Are you willing to travel?** Travel can impact your work-life balance and is definitely something to consider. Decide early on if this is something you want to commit to and ask for the estimated percentage of travel required.

- **Tell me about an accomplishment you are most proud of.** This is an easy question to prepare for; simply talk about your prior experience of something you accomplished. Maybe you tackled a large project or resolved an issue that allowed your company to save money, attract new customers, increase employee satisfaction, and so on.

- **Tell me about a time you made a mistake.** This is more difficult to answer. No one likes to highlight their mistakes. Have something ready to discuss and also be ready to explain how you fixed your mistake and the lessons you learned.

- **What is your dream job?** Be open here; talk about your likes and dislikes. Don't just say that this is the perfect role for you; really describe your dream job. From my experience, this has really worked well for me. I was applying for a job that included a dual role; half of it was incident response, and half was data analytics. When asked about my dream job, I was open and transparent and said that the incident response piece was really not for me and that I was truly passionate about data analytics. I'm so glad I said that, because apparently there was another job opening for a strictly data analytics manager!

- **Discuss your résumé.** This is something you should get good at doing. Just talk about your experience. I usually start with my current position and describe what I do now, and then I briefly summarize my past positions in chronological order.
- **Why should we hire you?** This is your elevator pitch, a thirty- to ninety-second spiel about why you are so awesome. What are your biggest strengths, and how can you start to add value immediately upon hire? Can you make the hiring manager's life easier? Tell them how you plan to do that. An elevator pitch should be well rehearsed while seeming to flow naturally. Avoid use of acronyms and incorporate your major competencies.
- **Why are you looking for a new job?** Are you just starting out? Are you looking for a change in career? Have a good story about why you are looking for a new job.
- **What are your salary requirements?** Know your value, and don't accept offers just because they are there; have a number in mind, and if the offer doesn't come close to that, then negotiate until you feel that you are receiving fair compensation. Conduct some research on average salaries to be prepared to negotiate. According to a survey conducted by O'Reilly, 2015 Data Science Salary Survey, "the median annual base salary of the survey sample is $91,000, and among US respondents is $104,000. The middle 50% of US respondents earn between $77,000 and $135,000."
- **What motivates you?** Are you motivated by money? Sense of accomplishment? Leading a team? Learning new skills?
- **What's your availability?** Are you able to start right away?
- **Can you talk about some models/dashboards you've built that relate to our needs?** This is something you should prepare for by reading the job description. Are there specific models that are discussed or use of specific methods, such as decision trees, Bayesian, random forests, or k-means? Do some research and think about similar work you've done that you can apply to those tasks. For example, one thing I personally did in interviews was, after we were done talking, following up with my interviewers and thanking them for their time; I also included a summary of the dashboards I've built (along with snapshots and descriptions).

This way they could get an idea of my quality of work and my knowledge.

- **What questions do you have for me?** Always have a few questions prepared so you show interest in the position. Some of my go-to questions that I have for interviewers are as follows:
  o Who will this position report to?
  o How many people are there on the team?
  o Is this position a new one, or is it open because someone left?
  o Why do you, the hiring manager, work here, and what's your favorite part of the job

No matter how much you prepare, there will always be some question that stumps you or just something you can't answer the way you would've wanted. Don't worry, and most importantly don't panic. You can always say you'll do some research and get back to them later. You can redeem yourself with the thank-you follow-up e-mail. Try your hardest, and talk about the logic you would use to approach a problem, if you don't know how to solve the problem that you are presented with.

Congratulations

If you are reading this page, then you have gotten through the entire book. Thank you!

I highly recommend that you spend a few minutes reading through the author bios and getting to know the amazing storytellers!

If you found value in the insights provided here, I would be extremely happy if you were to leave a review or send me an e-mail with your comments—kate@storybydata.com.

Thank you again for your time and attention!

AUTHOR'S BIOS

Huge thanks to all the people who were willing to participate in the informational interview process. Your input has truly made this book extremely valuable and insightful. It was great hearing about your experiences and advice.

Matt Williams

Matt Williams founded WD Creative Analytics in 2015, building a cross-functional team of data engineers, data scientists, and machine learning and artificial intelligence researchers to tackle automated metadata, video analytics, Fintech, and predictive algorithm modeling challenges.

Matt's focus is on narrative and meaning from analytics, and his background spans more than a decade in NLP and knowledge systems development, from scoring and weighted matching algorithms at LexisNexis, to classification, behavioral segmentation, and search architecture at Wyndham Worldwide, through audience and personalization systems demonstrations for Adobe.

WD Creative Analytics uses machine learning and cognitive techniques to derive meaning and value across structured and unstructured data sets in media, marketing, insurance, finance, research, and tech industries. Matt is leveraging a BA from Vassar College in cognitive science, synthesizing linguistics, psychology, and programming techniques to deliver innovative knowledge systems that link disparate data into a unified picture.

Matt has deployed a wide variety of machine-learning techniques during a career in data engineering, algorithms, and app development projects in data integration, enterprise search, analytics, and modeling.

Hector Alvaro Rojas

Hector Alvaro Rojas is a Data Science, Visualizations and Applied Statistics professional who holds a master in statistics, bachelor in statistics and a statistician title so far. He has more than fifteen years of experience as a consultant as well as formal work in private and public sectors and in the Academy as well. He has work experiences in both Chile and the United States.

He got into the field of data science as a natural continuation of his journey from the statistics field. His specialization in data science is been obtained in a preferably self-taught way, achieving a vision and updated knowledge of the development of this area both in its methodological component as well as in its more usual and direct applications. Hector is constantly acquiring new knowledge in data science and currently he has been focused on subjects such as R and Python Machine Learning and special Data Analytics, Web Scraping, Text Mining and Sentiment Analysis to later on facing the topics of Deep Learning and Big Data in its general context [Hadoop, Spark, MapReduce, PySpark, Hive, Pig, and so on ...]. He prefers using R, Python and SAS platforms, but he knows about SPSS and Excel enough to use them as a complementary support if needed. He uses Tableau as BI and visualization tool, he interacts among platforms by using HTML and he has played around a little bit with Amazon AWS free hosted data warehouse product.

Data science, Autodidact.
Master's degree in statistics, Pontificia Universidad Católica de Chile. Santiago, Chile.
Statistician, Universidad Austral de Chile. Valdivia, Chile.
Bachelor of science in statistics, Universidad Austral de Chile. Valdivia, Chile.

Mike Tamir

Mike serves as Takt Chief Data Science Officer, is part of the UC Berkeley iSchool Data Science faculty and sits on the advisory boards for several machine-learning projects, including Skymind/DL4J, Corvana, GameTime and InterTrust. Mike has led teams of data scientists in the Bay Area as chief data scientist for InterTrust, director of data sciences for MetaScale/Sears, and chief science officer for Galvanize, where he oversaw Galvanize's transformation into the premier data science and immersive education institution. He also founded the galvanizeU-UNH accredited master of science in data science degree. Mike began his career in academia serving as a mathematics teaching fellow for Columbia University before teaching at the University of Pittsburgh. His early research focused on developing the epsilon-anchor methodology for resolving both an inconsistency he highlighted in the dynamics of Einstein's general relativity theory and the convergence of "large N" Monte Carlo simulations in statistical mechanics' universality models of criticality phenomena.

Alexander Bessonov

Built and deployed models to forecast various timeseries data. Led development of HBasebased graph database and RESTful microservices utilizing the database and Cloudera Search (Solr). Led development of streaming graph visualization web app (based on D3.js, Sigma.js and Oboe.js). Designed and implemented entity resolution algorithms and frameworks for SNA project using Apache Spark GraphX.

Implemented R and Python packages to help data analysts to obtain required data. Implemented frameworks to run R and Python code on Hadoop cluster. Implemented web scrapers for structured and semistructured data. Deployed several external data acquisition pipelines.

Designed and implemented data analytics architecture for an anti-fraud project using Python OLAP framework, Neo4j, and PostrgreSQL. Contributed to OSS projects. Implemented several web scrapers to extract media resources, user profile information, product prices, URLs, and so on.

Education:

Moscow Power Engineering Institute (Technical University)

- Master's degree, electronic systems, 2006
- Thesis topic: Automatic number plate recognition

Mansi Gupta

I was a BITS Pilani undergraduate, tackling spam at LinkedIn. My passion lies in using the power of data science to make this world a better place. My research interests are focused in the areas of NLP and machine learning.

I pursued my undergraduate degree in computer science from Birla Institute of Technology and Science, Pilani, and graduated in 2015. During graduation, I pursued electives such as machine learning and advanced data science and projects related to information retrieval, social media mining, and machine-learning techniques, which initiated me into the field of data science.

Vaibhav Gedigeri

As it is said, "Torture the data, and it will confess to anything!"

My story so far…

Simply put, I juggle data to make things beautiful!

With my diverse background in schooling, I completed my bachelor's degree in computer science with a focus in artificial intelligence from VTU. A logical extension to my interests landed me in the Garden State, New Jersey, where I have completed my master's degree with a focus in machine learning from Stevens Institute of Technology.

My stint as a data scientist, first at Prognos (a clinical lab intelligence firm) and then at Dun & Bradstreet, provided me the foundation to go on to join Honeywell as a data scientist, where we leverage the power IIOT data to improve the wide range of products.

I am a travel enthusiast, a soccer player on weekends, and a Manchester United fan at heart! I am also pianist by hobby and an avid learner.

Charles Givre

Mr. Charles Givre has worked as a senior lead data scientist for Booz Allen Hamilton for the last six years, where he works in the intersection of cybersecurity and data science. For the last few years, Mr. Givre worked on one of Booz Allen's largest analytic programs, where he led data science efforts and worked to expand the role of data science in the program.

Mr. Givre is passionate about teaching others data science and analytic skills and has taught data science classes all over the world at conferences, at universities, and for clients. Most recently, Mr. Givre taught a data science class at the BlackHat conference in Las Vegas and the Center for Research in Applied Cryptography and Cyber Security at Bar Ilan University. He is a sought-after speaker and has delivered presentations at major industry conferences such as Strata-Hadoop World, BlackHat, Open Data Science Conference, and others.

One of Mr. Givre's research interests is increasing the productivity of data science and analytic teams, and toward that end, he has been working extensively to promote the use of Apache Drill in security applications and has contributed to the code base. Mr. Givre teaches online classes for O'Reilly about Drill and security data science and is a coauthor for the forthcoming O'Reilly book about Apache Drill.

Prior to joining Booz Allen, Mr. Givre worked as a counterterrorism analyst at the Central Intelligence Agency for five years. Mr. Givre holds a master's degree in Middle Eastern studies from Brandeis University, as well as a bachelor of science in computer science and a bachelor of music, both from the University of Arizona. Mr. Givre holds various certifications, including CISSP, Security+, Network+, Certified Penetration Tester, and CDIA+. He speaks French reasonably well, plays the trombone, and lives in Baltimore with his family. In his nonexistent spare time, he is restoring a classic British sports car. Mr. Givre blogs at thedataist.com and tweets @cgivre.

John Bottega

John Bottega is a senior strategy and data management executive with more than thirty-five years of experience in the industry. Over his career, John has held various positions in supporting a firm's data management functions. From 2006 to 2014, John held the title of chief data officer in both the private and public sectors, serving as CDO for Citibank and Bank of America, and holding the post of CDO for the Federal Reserve Bank of New York. Today, John is the principal and managing member of his own consulting firm, Data Management

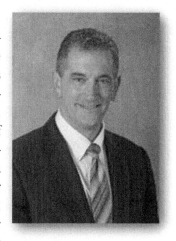

Advisory Services, LLC, and is senior advisor and consultant for the Enterprise Data Management Council, where he is responsible for the council's CDO Forum and Data Management Best Practices activity and their Data Capability Assessment Model (DCAM) training program.

As the former chief data officer at Bank of America, John was responsible for driving the enterprise data management strategy. This included championing the data management policy and standards; establishing and operationalizing data governance; working with technology to define the data platform, infrastructure, and tool simplification; and supporting the bank's data scientist team in their efforts to drive improved information analytics.

As the chief data officer for the Federal Reserve Bank of New York (FRBNY), John worked with domestic and foreign regulators on financial sector data management and data quality. While at FRBNY, John led the effort to define and establish the LEI (Legal Entity Identifier), a global information standard for unique entity identification, key to enabling and strengthening systemic risk analysis in support of global financial stability. John also served as a senior advisor to the director of the Office of Financial Research (OFR), an agency established by the Dodd-Frank Act within the US Department of the Treasury, responsible for the analysis and monitoring of industry-wide systemic risk.

As chief data officer for Citigroup's Corporate and Investment Banking, John defined their data management improvement strategy and road map. He led an effort that reduced the bank's BASEL capital risk exposure through improved data quality initiatives, resulting in significant bottom-line savings to the firm.

John has been a frequent speaker for more than seventeen years at industry conferences and industry symposiums. He is currently a member of the US Treasury Department's Financial Research Advisory Committee to the OFR, a member of the Executive Advisory Board of NewVantage Partners, a member of the Wall Street & Technology Reader Advisory Board, and a member of the Board of Directors of ACTUS, a nonprofit association focused on the improvement of systemic risk monitoring and financial market transparency.

June Andrews

June Andrews is a principal data scientist at Wise/GE Digital, working on machine learning and data science platform for the Industrial Internet of Things, which includes aviation, trains, and power plants.

Previously, she worked at Pinterest, spearheading the Data Trustworthiness and Signals Program to create a healthy data ecosystem for Pinterest's machine learning. She has also worked as technical lead and staff data scientist at LinkedIn, specializing in growth, engagement, and social network analysis with the goal of increasing economic opportunity for professionals.

Additional experiences include search at Yelp, data consulting for a health-care start-up, and analyzing the structure of voting and publication networks with John Hopcroft. June holds degrees in applied mathematics, computer science, and electrical engineering from UC Berkeley and Cornell.

Sergey Bryl

Sergey is a Data Scientist at a software product company MacPaw. After spending nearly 12 years working as an analyst in bank industry, he switched to e-commerce and marketing analytics. Then, he worked in the online gaming industry as a Data Scientist. Highly self-organized, lifelong learner and blogger (analyzecore.com) with high attention to details and ability to understand business problems. He always tries to do analytics actionable and helpful.

LinkedIn profile: https://www.linkedin.com/in/sergeybryl/

Kunal Jain

Kunal Jain, founder of Analytics Vidhya, is an IIT Bombay graduate and has eight years of global business analytics experience. His work experience ranges from mature markets such as the United Kingdom to developing markets such as India.

In his last engagement before starting up, he had set up and scaled up a business analytics and intelligence team in a multinational Insurance company.

Always keen to learn the next technological disruption, he can have passionate discussions about gadgets, automobiles, technology, and health (although the amount of discussions on health has no correlation with his own fitness!) at any time of the day.

Renee M. P. Teate

I am a creative data scientist with strong communication skills.

As a data generalist working at a start-up, I work on several teams and contribute to a variety of projects at HelioCampus, including but not limited to predictive analytics/data science, Tableau dashboard design and development, SQL for data extraction and preparation, data visualization research, and social media contribution.

I have an undergraduate degree in integrated science and technology from James Madison University.

I have been the co-owner and vice president of a small database/web/software development company for over ten years, where I've been lead developer and database designer.

Khalifeh Al Jadda, PhD

Khalifeh Al Jadda holds a PhD in computer science from the University of Georgia (UGA), with a specialization in machine learning.

He has experience implementing large-scale distributed machine-learning algorithms to solve challenging problems in domains ranging from bioinformatics to search and recommendation engines. He is the lead data scientist on the search data science team at CareerBuilder, which is one of the largest job boards in the world.

He leads the data science effort to design and implement the back-end of CareerBuilder's language-agnostic semantic search engine leveraging Apache Spark and the Hadoop ecosystem. He is also the founder and chairman of the Data Science Council at CareerBuilder, which organizes events and hosts prominent speakers to promote data science in the Atlanta community.

Diane Reynolds

As the chief data scientist at IBM, Diane is responsible for the data science inside the industry solutions for the financial services sector. She focuses mainly on client insights for wealth managers and retail banking. One of the new solutions, RCA (Regulatory Compliance Analytics), is a cloud-based solution that reads and interprets banking regulations by leveraging IBM's Watson APIs. It's an invigorating, innovative environment with lots of challenges, unknowns, and learning opportunities.

Sean Preusse

Hands-on product manager and data science consultant, passionate about solving complex business problems and working with senior leaders and customers to define the vision and build value. Proven experience in leading a team of analysts within highly complex and changing environments.

Developed analytics vision and road map with the redesign of most analytical products and the introduction of new processes and tools, such as Python, Tableau, GitHub, Jira, Confluence, R, Hadoop, D3, and Capability Sessions.

Commercialize strategic workforce analytics across the employee lifecycle. Finalist, Analytical Excellence. Teradata EPIC Awards, Partners Conference 2016, Atlanta. Led and delivered value on a multilayered analytics data pipeline and analytical record.

Developed predictive models to better understand the relationship of the workforce to improve customer service and employee well-being. Recognition from the CEO on well-being predictive analytics and intervention. 2016 Pinnacle HR High Achiever Award.

Hands on and experienced in SQL, Python, R, Tableau across rapid prototyping, scientific packages, and effective dashboard and visualization design principals.

Andrew Paul Acosta

Knowledge of finance and statistics, optimization theory, statistical analysis (causality modeling and Bayesian networks), and enterprise risk analysis. Experience with numerical analysis packages and scripting languages. Association for Computing Machinery (ACM) senior member.

In-depth knowledge of big data predictive analysis, including relational data mining, neural network, nearest k-neighbors, association rules, time series, regression trees, sequence clustering, and Naïve Bayes.

Expertise in power market risk model analytics of PJM and other ISO/RTO markets, including peak/off-peak load analysis, using day-ahead and real-time market data of power generation, transmission, and congestion at various LMP zones/hubs.

Professional speaker invited to deliver presentations in economic theory, finance, econometrics, financial regulation, trading strategies, biostatistics, and information systems management. University graduate-level finance and information systems instructor.

Deep experience in the analysis of financial market data in researching fixed-income instruments and derivatives, especially mortgage products.

Armando Vieira

Entrepreneur, scientist, and machine-learning enthusiast.

Recently engaged in applying deep learning networks for hard problems on classification and regression.

Writing a book, titled *Business Applications of Deep Learning*, to be released in 2017. More info on my website: armando.lidinwise.com.

Author of more than seventy publications in international journals such as *Expert Systems with Applications, Journal of Applied Physics, Neurocomputing,* and *Physical Review E.* Cocreator of a new algorithm to classify high-dimensional data (HLVQ).

More on ResearchGate profile: https://www.researchgate.net/profile/Armando_Vieira3

Passionate and experienced with predictive analytics and big data using machine-learning approaches such as support vector machines, complex networks analysis, and artificial neural networks.

Great degree of autonomy, comfortable in handling ambiguity, and at ease in translating business requirements into algorithms and algorithms into value. Have coordinated several projects on credit risk evaluation, recommendation systems, clustering analysis, and predictive analytics.

Raj Bandyopadhyay

I am the director of Data Science Education at Springboard. My goal is to keep our data science curriculum up to date, based on student and mentor feedback and ongoing industry trends. I'd also like to create and nurture a community of badass data science industry mentors.

Previously, I was the chief data scientist at Pindrop Security. I improved the risk scoring formula for phone calls using a data-driven approach to reduce the false positive rate. For the biggest financial client, this new formula reduced the false positive rate by 40 percent, thereby saving fraud analyst time required to review those calls.

I developed an algorithm to analyze call detail record (CDR) data and interactive voice response (IVR) state information to detect reconnaissance activity in IVR systems that serve as an early warning of fraud (specifically, account takeover) attempts. I presented this work at BlackHat 2014 and obtained a provisional patent. This work is currently being productized at Pindrop and being tested with development partners.

I improved Phone Reputation Service (PRS) algorithm to detect phone spam (i.e., telemarketing and other unwanted calls), which has resulted in sales of the service to several new customers.

Rosaria Silipo

Dr. Rosaria Silipo holds a master's degree in electrical engineering from the University of Florence (Italy, 1992) and a doctorate title in bioengineering from the Politecnico di Milano (Italy, 1996). The doctorate work dealt with statistical and machine-learning algorithms for the automatic analysis of the electrocardiographic signal and was developed at the University of Florence (Italy) in cooperation with the Massachusetts Institute of Technology (USA).

She has been awarded two postdoctoral fellowships: one at Siemens (Munich, Germany, 1996–1997) and one at ICSI at the University of Berkeley (USA, 1997–2000) for the automatic analysis of biomedical signals and speech.

In 2000, she moved into the corporate world as a research engineer at Nuance (Menlo Park, USA, 2000–2002); as a senior developer at Spoken Translation (Berkeley, USA, 2002–2007); and as the manager of the SAS development group at Viseca (Zurich, Switzerland, 2007–2009).

Using the extensive experience acquired over the past years in applying data mining algorithms to industrial products, in 2009 she became a data mining consultant, helping companies to organize, clean, and finally make sense of their data. From time to time, she cooperates with KNIME in the development of cutting edge predictive analytics applications.

Rosaria Silipo is the author of more than fifty scientific publications and three books for data analysis practitioners.

Ben Taylor

I watch the watchers; I direct the learners.

I am passionate about machine learning. My life's mission is to further the boundaries of what is possible with data science. I spend as much time as I can working with deep learning, NLP, and all forms of data science. I currently have a passion project I am managing in which I am combining the power of genetic programming with deep learning to automate network design. I think there is a trend happening in data science in which human expertise and creativity are being replaced by powerful new methods (e.g., deep learning, big data).

I am most well known for my machine-learning work with the data science community and with HireVue. With the community, I enjoy posting opinions on jobs and tutorials on ML methods. I also enjoy speaking and presenting to all types of audiences. I joined HireVue as their first data scientist and was able to partner with engineering to build out one of the first video interview prediction engines, called HireVue Insights. Since starting there, I have been able to help build out a data science team, and together we "boldly go where no man has gone before." That product has been out for the past two years and has seen fantastic use cases and growth with large Fortune companies dramatically reducing time to hire from six weeks to six days. I love my machine-learning journey and the bizarre twisted path I took to get where I am today.

Steven Tedjamulia

Steven Tedjamulia is the CEO and cofounder of Predictive Science. Prior to Predictive Science, Steven was the founder and executive practice lead for Dell's Digital Strategy and Innovation consulting practice, where he was responsible for providing strategic consulting services to Fortune 1000 marketers such as Carnival Cruise Lines, Equinox, and VMware.

Steven also served as the director and cofounder of Dell's digital and social commerce innovation labs, where he led strategic efforts in creating, experimenting, partnering, and launching digital and big data technologies. Growing his team from 1 to 130 people, Steve raised $18 million, launched over fifty digital projects, and formed an advisory board that included Reid Hoffman (Greylock, Linkedin), Jim Breyer (Accel), Jim Goetz (Sequoia), Bing Gordon (KPCM), Maynard Webb (LiveOps), Sheryl Sandberg (Facebook), and Jeff Weiner (Linkedin). He secured thirteen patents, created a Dell subsidiary company called Marketvine, sold over $2 million in products, and helped drive the development of Dell's big data initiatives.

Steven spent more than ten years working as a general manager, product manager, and business development manager at Bazaarvoice, Open Text, Vignette, Collanos, Novell, and Brigham Young University. He serves on boards of Brand Innovators, Digital Strategy Innovation Summit, Chief Strategy Officer Magazine, and Tech Media.

Jared P. Lander

Jared Lander is the chief data scientist of Lander Analytics, a data science consultancy based in New York City, the organizer of the New York Open Statistical Programming Meetup and the New York R Conference, and an adjunct professor of statistics at Columbia University.

With a master's degree from Columbia University in statistics and a bachelor's degree from Muhlenberg College in mathematics, he has experience in both academic research and industry. His work for both large and small organizations ranges from music and fund raising to finance and humanitarian relief efforts.

He specializes in data management, multilevel models, machine learning, generalized linear models, data management, and statistical computing. He is the author of *R for Everyone: Advanced Analytics and Graphics*, a book about R programming geared toward data scientists and nonstatisticians alike and is creating a course on glmnet with DataCamp.

David Rubal

David is the group vice president of Oracle's North America Public Sector Cloud and Infrastructure Solutions Sales Engineering organization. David is a senior technology executive with more than thirty-five years of sales engineering experience spanning multiple global market segments and verticals, including federal, state, and local governments.

Prior to joining Oracle, David held technology and executive leadership positions with Blue Coat Systems, Tableau Software, EMC, Cisco, and others. David is the principal coauthor of the 2009 White House OMB "Planning Guide/Roadmap Toward IPv6 Adoption within the US Government" artifact.

As a recognized industry thought leader, David shares his vision and strategies in social media and as an executive speaker on key government technology initiatives, including big data, analytics, cloud computing, cyber security, FedRAMP, and smart cities.

SOURCES CITED:

Thomas H. DavenportD.J. Patil "Data Scientist: The Sexiest Job of the 21st Century" FROM THE OCTOBER 2012 ISSUE. https://hbr.org/2012/10/data-scientist-the-sexiest-job-of-the-21st-century

Springboard "Ultimate Guide to Data Science Interview".https://www.springboard.com/blog/wp-content/uploads/2016/07/UltimateGuidetoDataScienceInterviews-1.pdf

Jacquelyn Smith, FORBES "How To Ace The 50 Most Common Interview Questions".http://www.forbes.com/sites/jacquelyn-smith/2013/01/11/how-to-ace-the-50-most-common-interview-questions/#66eb26b74873

John King & Roger Magoulas, O'Reilly "2015 Data Science Salary Survey". https://duu8606n09pv.cloudfront.net/reports/2015-data-science-salary-survey.pdf

Kate Strachnyi

This book was compiled by Kate Strachnyi.

Kate is a manager working for Deloitte; focused on risk management, governance, and regulatory response solutions for financial services organizations.

She is currently working in the data visualization space. She previously served as an insights strategy manager and research analyst, where she was responsible for enabling the exchange of information in an efficient and timely manner.

Prior to consulting, she worked for the chief risk officer of a full-service commercial bank, where she was in charge of developing an ERM program, annual submission of ICAAP, and gap analysis of Basel II/III directives. Additionally, she worked as a business development associate at the Global Association of Risk Professionals (GARP).

Kate received a bachelor of business administration in finance and investments from Baruch College, Zicklin School of Business. Certifications include Project Management Professional (PMP) and Tableau Desktop 10 Qualified Associate.

E-mail: kate@storybydata.com

Twitter: @StoryByData

Blog: http://storybydata.com/

Made in the USA
Coppell, TX
30 April 2020

23568737R00075